Leadership & Development

Abathar Tajaldeen

Jalal Moughania

Authors: Abathar Tajaldeen and Jalal Moughania

Published by: The Mainstay Foundation

© 2017 The Mainstay Foundation

Printed in the United States.

ISBN: 978-1943393541

To our Beloved Twelfth Imam.

CONTENTS

PREFACE

It was an honor and pleasure to work on this project of adapting some of the writings of Sayyid Sadiq Alkhersan on human development, ethics, and leadership. His writings provided great insight into the principles of human development in accordance to the Holy Quran and the Prophet Muhammad. It was truly amazing to see how deep and insightful the Sayyid's work was on this crucial subject.

This book is based on a number of Sayyid Alkhersan's works which we adapted into one volume. In particular, we relied on the following publications:

- *Al-Rasul al-A'tham wa al-Tanmiya al-Bashariya (The Grand Prophet and Human Development)*
- *Usus al-'Adala 'ind al-Imam 'Ali (Imam Ali and the Principles of Justice)*
- *Usus al-Nazaha: Qira'a fi Wasiyat al-Imam al-Hussain (The Principles of Integrity: A Study of the Sermon of Imam Hussain)*

- *Al-Imam al-Sadiq wa al-Tandheer li al-Altanmiya al-Bashariya (Imam Sadiq and the Theory of Human Development)*

As each of these works approached the topic of human development from a unique perspective and added valuable historical insight, we found that weaving them together into a single book would provide the greatest value.

Before our readers begin this book, we hope that they keep a few important points in mind.

Firstly, the process of translation always begs us to find precise meanings for the passages that we translate. But when we encounter the majesty of the Holy Quran, we find ourselves incapable of understanding its intricacies, let alone translating its true and deep meanings. We turned to the works of translators who have attempted to do this before. Although no translation can do justice to the Holy Quran, we found that the translation of Ali Quli Qarai to be the most proper in understanding when compared to the interpretation of the text as derived by our grand scholars. As such, we decided to rely on Qarai's translations throughout this book, with minor adaptations that allowed us to weave the verses more properly with the rest of the work.

A second great limitation came with translating the narrations of the Grand Prophet Muhammad and his Holy Household (Peace Be Upon Them). Their words are ever so deep and ever so powerful. We attempted to convey these passages to the reader in a tone that is understandable without deviating from the essence of the words of these immaculate personalities. We pray that we were successful in this endeavor.

Finally, we want to take this opportunity to thank you for your support. As students of Islam and as authors of this text, our greatest purpose is to please God by passing along these teachings to others. By picking up this book, you have lent your crucial support to this endeavor. We hope that you will continue your support throughout the rest of this book, and we ask that you keep us in your prayers whenever you pick it up.

Abathar Tajaldeen & Jalal Moughania,

The Mainstay Foundation

PROLOGUE

Islam looks at the idea of human development as continuous movement through the lifetime of a human being. Development serves the purpose of man in his strive for excellence and perfection. It is part and parcel to the life of a Muslim and naturally should be a driving force in the life of every human being. Without acknowledging it, learning how to use it, and incorporating it in one's life, there is surely something missing. It is the gateway to excellent leadership, whether it is in one's home, organization, or community. The concepts of leadership and development go hand in hand, as shown to us by the Holy Prophet Muhammad (pbuh) and his disciples.

The origins of human development commenced in humanity's nascent years as mankind attempted to understand the changes that surrounded them. It was the natural result of the observation and contemplation man engaged in relation to the changes in his environment – in the revolutions of seasons and nature, plants and wildlife, and mankind. These constant natural changes demonstrated that this world is in enduring continuous transformation.

These observations and contemplations led to the rise of philosophical discourse with respect to the inherent essence of worldy objects and the natural changes that occurred within them. The ancient Greek philosophers were the first to initiate such discourse in Europe, and prominent among them was a man named Heraclitus. He focused immensely on change in the universe, indicating that the world is in a constant state of motion and transformation. Heraclitus became famously known for saying, "You can never step into the same river twice." His theory stated that everything in the universe is perpetually in flux.

Parmenides rejected Heraclitus' theory. He believed that reality is singular and true change is impossible. Plato's theory also opposed Heraclitus' philosophy. Plato believed that change is a physical phenomenon and reality cannot be ascertained except through form or thought. Form and thought, said Plato, are not subject to change as it is only through them that we discern what is real.

Aristotle discussed the concept of change from a different angle. He stated that in the study of organisms, we find a system of movement from one stage to the next. It commences with birth, then moves to maturity, and concludes with decay. In each stage of growth, there is a sense of desire for the upcoming stage. Every stage is embedded with the potential energy for the next stage.

In the 14th century, a prominent Arab intellectual and sociologist by the name of Abdulrahman Ibn Khaldun had new ideas on the topic. He gave the concept of social change a broader scope that was more comprehensive than his predecessors. Ibn Khaldun emphasized that social phenomenon does not arise from nowhere. To understand a social occurrence, we need to be cognizant of the environment in which it took place. Ibn Khaldun attributed the behavior and lifestyle of a person to the profession he had in his community. That job served to fulfilled his basic needs in its most fundamental sense. The jobs assumed and the needs present are the cause for people's collaboration, networking, and community building.

Ibn Khaldun explained his ideas as follows,

> *The difference in the circumstances amongst generations is due to the differences in what they earn with regards to their livelihood. They associate so they can help one another attain sustenance and start by concentrating on garnering necessities... before wants and accessories... and it was their association and collaboration for their needs, livelihood, and securing food, shelter, and warmth... It was only for what is necessary to preserve their lives and provide the basic essentials of life, without any excess to be stored for future shortages. Then if the circumstances of those seeking earnings for livelihood improved, and they exceeded their needs,*

and have an excess in wealth and [enjoy] prosperity, they
would become tranquil and benevolent.[1]

Ibn Khaldun's theory on change within society was focused on the practical causes and implications of people. It was based on the need to survive and the need to grow. After the demise of Ibn Khaldun and until the early beginnings of the Renaissance in Europe, there was no noteworthy advancements related to the study of human development. The sweeping developments and revolutions in thought, religion, politics, and economics which ensued resulted in expansive advancement in the study of humanities. Philosophical discourse reached its prime during the 18th century, and rendered the emergence of new theories in development, advancement, and progressiveness. Novel philosophies about the universe and life became prominent. Because contemporary theories on human development are closely connected to the theories and thoughts during that era, looking at some of the major incidents and ideas associated with the Renaissance helps provide a context of the subject matter of this book.

Even though one cannot ascertain precisely the transition from Medieval Times to the Renaissance, it is fair to say that it was partly inspired by the Arab-Islamic civilization. Through the research and findings of Arab scientists and philosophers, Europe was exposed to new ideas and slowly began to wake up from its intellectual coma with the advent

---

[1] Ibn Khaldun, Al-Muqaddimah, 1:120.

of the 13th century. Frederik II, Holy Roman Emperor and King of Sicily during the Middle Ages, established a marketplace for literature, science, and philosophy in Sicily. He would invite renowned Arab philosophers to this marketplace to share their work and publications. Moreover, Frederik II established two schools, one for sciences in Napoli and a second for medicine in Salerno. From these two schools, a university in Paris was founded. Soon, Paris became the desired destination for many European students. Following some developments, some English students left the school and returned back home to build a new private university, what would become the world renowned Oxford University.

During the 13th century, Europe witnessed remarkable advancement in literature and philosophy. English philosopher Roger Bacon entered the limelight. He rejected the notion that things are created the way we perceive them. He proposed that natural phenomenon have explanations that we need to explore. He was accused of atheism, persecuted, and condemned by the Church.[2] It is through the works of such individuals, generation after generation of intellectual discourse and development, that the concept of human development would grow.

Development became one of the most important concepts in the 20th century. This term was coined to describe the process of establishing robust political and economic sys-

---

[2] See: *Arab Global Encyclopedia*, "Development."

tems. It became known as "The Process of Development". The concept was indicative of the transformation that was evident in Asia and Africa with the decline of colonialism after World War II, and the decline of communism thereafter, in the 1960s.

The notion of development becomes increasingly important because of its various dimensions as it pertains to cultural strategy, production, and progress. Though the term was introduced during the time of the renowned economist and thinker Adam Smith in the 18th century, it was scarcely used until after World War II. The terms that were commonly used to refer to development were "material progress" and "economic progress". Even in light of the economic movement in eastern Europe in the 19th century, the terms frequently employed were "modernization" and "industrialization".

The term "development" was actually first used in economics. It was coined to refer to the process of implementing a host of root changes in a specific community with an objective to empower the community to continuously advance such that it ensures growth and prosperity for all of its members. In other words, strengthening the ability of the community to fulfill the primary needs and the increasing wants of its constituents. The objective is to raise the ability of the community to fulfill the needs of its members through consistent education on how to efficiently utilize available resources and manage effective distribution.

Next, the concept of development traveled to the political arena in the sixth decade of the 20th century. It formed as an independent term referring to the advancement of non-European countries towards democracy. "Political development" became defined as a process of multi-dimensional social change with an objective to reach the position of industrial countries. What is meant by the "position of industrial countries" is establishing multiple systems that can render economic growth, voter participation, and political competition, and can champion the values of citizenship, sovereignty, and patriotism to one's nation.

Onward, the usage of the term increased and found its way in many other fields. It became more prevalent in cultural development which sought to elevate the level of education in the community. It surfaced in social development which aimed to advance the social interactions between the various community players – individuals, groups, organizations, private foundations and government. In addition to all of this, the concept of human development was particularly brought to the forefront. This notion of development was concerned with supporting the potential of the individual, measuring his standard of living, and improving his conditions in the community.[3]

The idea of human development moved on to encompass a wide range of fields including administration, politics, culture, and education. The individual is the common denomi-

---

[3] The preceding five paragraphs were adapted from Dr. Nasr Aref, *The concept of development*, College of Political Science – University of Cairo. (pg. 35.)

nator in all of these fields. When frameworks and structures in administration, politics, and education improve, they have direct effects on the development of the individual with respect to his skills, values, and engagement. The individual becomes a beneficiary of the development. Human development is the cornerstone that strategists and decision makers rely on to prepare the proper conditions for social and economic progress. In conclusion, we can broadly define human development as a course interested in improving the quality of human resources, while improving the quality of the individual. Human development in Islam, however, is more encompassing.

Islam emphasized that human development is meant for, and is driven by, individuals, because of their dynamic personalities, ever increasing body of knowledge, and endless potential. Development is an incentive for diligence, persistence, excellence, precision, and other facets of growth. Comprehensive growth that affects and is effected by the movement of society. Consequently, human development is not novel in Islam, although it was not coined as a term of art until recently.

The Islamic concept preceded others. The solidity of concepts such as "love" and "good morals" became the springboard for human development that aimed to advance people. In its material and moral dimensions, it provided the human a sustainable opportunity for growth, not only through improving the Earth, developing cities, and launching commercial projects,[4] but also through strengthening the society so development can become the nucleus for optimal investment in the intangible abilities and potentials of people.

Outside of Islam, it can be argued that the concept of human development was reduced to increasing people's standard of living and potential wealth. It came down to how people can better themselves to have a better standard of living, and in turn contribute in a greater way to the development of society's economic prosperity. Islam's approach to human development is different in its focus on the individual's intellectual and spiritual dimensions not merely as tools for their material gain in economic terms. Acknowledging all facets of the human being, the Islamic approach naturally became more compatible with an individuals' reality. It instills the spirit of responsibility in man and energizes him to strive for his rights and ambitions, pursuing a balance of prosperity for this life and the next. The Holy Prophet refers to this in his statement below.

> *God says 'By My Might and Majesty and my ascension to the top of My Throne, if people from a tribe, household, or the desert, who were engaged in sinning that I abhor and then changed to obedience that I love, [then] I will surely transform [their condition] from what they detest from My Punishment to what they love from My Mercy.*

---

[4] Wikipedia contributors, "Sustainable development," *Wikipedia, The Free Encyclopedia* (accessed August 2016).

And if people from a tribe, household, or the desert, who were engaged in obedience that I love and then changed to sinning that I abhor, [then] I will surely transform [their condition] from what they love from My Mercy to what they detest from My Wrath.[5]

As part of God's laws of existence, a person's ability to instill change is contingent on the strength of his will and dedication. In order to effectuate change, one must engage with the matter physically and mentally, and implement steps of reform and advancement. The will of the individuals leads to collective community will, one individual at a time. It is this collective strength that will uplift the community, and utilize its abilities and invest in its potentials.

God says, "Eat and drink, be not extravagant."[6] This is a directive for people to manage their consumption and spending so they do not become wasteful and avoid financial struggle. This verse, like the next, demonstrates a simple practical initiative to championing real development. "Do not devour your property among yourselves falsely, except that it be trading by your mutual consent."[7] In this verse, the Holy Quran is warning people from overconsuming their money and instead to encourage investments in trade that can render benefit to oneself and the community.

The Prophet focused particularly on trade stressing its importance when he said, "Nine-tenths of sustenance is in

---

[5] Al-Siyouti, *Al-Dur Al-Manshour*, 4:48.
[6] The Holy Quran, 7:31.
[7] The Holy Quran, 4:29.

trade." Trade and business bring tremendous benefit. It provides jobs for families. If people are employed, they will generate income that they can spend to stimulate the markets and grow the economy. Economic growth will help eliminate unemployment which is a source for numerous social diseases. Trade is the catalyst that activates this positive cycle. Additionally, the Prophet points to the importance of utilizing resources and investing in them using the proper guidelines. This also contributes to the growth of the economy.

The prosperity of the economy also helps people on a personal level. For example, when a merchant is working hard and occupied with his trade, he is less likely to fall to the ails of laziness, boredom, intervening in people's business, and any other trouble. When focused on his work, he will likely not have time or care to engage in disruptive thinking and or host negative thoughts of others.

Equally important is agricultural development, which is considered to be a great blessing in the grand scheme of community and society. God provided crops and animals as vital resources for mankind. It is an integral part of the sustenance that we seek and work for. The Holy Quran speaks about this blessing in several verses. In Surat Al-Araf, He states, 'Certainly We have established you in the Earth and made in it means of livelihood for you; little it is that you give thanks."[8] In another chapter God says,

---

[8] The Holy Quran, 7:10.

The Earth, We have spread it forth and made in it firm mountains and caused to grow in it of every suitable thing. We have made in it means of subsistence for you and for him for whom you are not the suppliers. There is not a thing but with Us are the treasures of it, and We do not send it down but in a known measure. We send the winds fertilizing, then send down water from the clouds, so We give it to you to drink of, nor is it you who store it up.[9]

After speaking about the important blessings, God instructs us in the Holy Quran to give and offer from that which He bestowed upon us.

Spend benevolently of the good things that you earn and or what We have brought forth for you out of the earth, and do not aim at what is bad that you may spend (in alms) of it, while you would not take it yourselves unless you have its price lowered, and know that God is Self-sufficient, Praiseworthy.[10]

There are other verses in the Holy Quran that speak about social development and change which is for the benefit of man. For example, God states, "Help one another in goodness and piety."[11] In another verse He declares,

Those who made their abode in the city and in the faith before them love those who have fled to them, and do not find in their hearts a need of what they are given, and prefer

---

9 The Holy Quran, 7:19-22.
10 The Holy Quran, 2:267.
11 The Holy Quran, 5:2.

*[them] before themselves though poverty may afflict them,
and whoever is preserved from the darkness of his soul, these
it is that are the successful ones.*[12]

These words urge Muslims to foster strong connections amongst each other and to build a community for all. This is essentially the goal of all humanity. The cohesion between people will render administrative and economic development which works for the progress of society. People will feel a sense of ownership and responsibility for the collective wellbeing and prosperity that is produced. This commitment for working for the common good brings stability with respect to security, economy, and general society. Furthermore, it gives all an opportunity to participate and contribute to the growth of their community. Those with experience and wisdom can comfortably help guide the direction of the community with better processes and ideas that will render harmonious benefit to the collective.

"Take counsel with them in the affair; so when you have decided, then place your trust in God; surely God loves those who trust."[13] These verses emphasize the importance of dialogue and engaging everyone in critical decisions. It is imperative to involve the different parties in decision-making and to consult and seek advice in effort to seek the best decision. This spirit of embracing the collective thought and working for the common good is what ought to perpetuate in society.

---

[12] The Holy Quran, 59:9.
[13] The Holy Quran, 3:159.

It is from this spirit that we engage in the discourse outlined in this book, with the purpose of contributing to culture of positive leadership and development. This book highlights principles in leadership and development that are integral for the growth and progress as individuals, and evidently as a collective community. As evidenced thus far, the inspiration here comes from the guidance of the Holy Quran, prophetic tradition, as well as building off the context of those that have come before us. It is our hope that this brief work helps to provide insight and inspiration for the reader interested in his or her development, and the development of his or her community.

DEVELOPMENT ORDAINED

God says in the Holy Quran, "We have sent down the Book to you as a clarification of all things and as guidance, mercy and good news for the Muslims,"[1] and that, "We have not omitted anything from the Book."[2] The verses refer to the truth that the Quran reveals in things, in that it is a book of guidance and mercy. It does this through its comprehensive calls to piety, integrity, good dealings, and virtuous manners with all those that we engage with. The Quran calls on us to always do what is better, and if possible, to do what is best. Thus, it is truly good news and glad tidings to those who work with it, as it guides them to the path of salvation and makes discovering that path so much easier for them. In the end it is glad tidings to all of humanity. The Holy Quran's guidance adds value and meaning to life. The qualities and characteristics it holds supports the growth and advancement of humanity in its pursuit for excellence and perfec-

---

[1] The Holy Quran, 16:89.
[2] The Holy Quran, 6:38.

tion. Such a book was sent and delivered through the noble Prophet of Islam, who is described as

> *The most beloved of prophets to Him, the most noble amongst them, is Muhammad ibn Abdullah... God chose him, favored him, and selected him... He gave him the keys of knowledge, the springs of wisdom, and sent him as a mercy to mankind and a [rain of mercy] to the lands...*[3]
> *He sent him with the illuminating light, the manifest proof, the apparent approach, and the guiding book...*[4]
> *[God] sent him as people were lost in mayhem, swayed in confusion, led by the reins of demise, and their hearts sealed by rusted locks...*[5]

The condition of reaching the treasure was following its guardian and protector. The one whose position is described by God's word, "O Prophet! Indeed, We have sent you as a witness, as a bearer of good news and as a warner and as a summoned to God by His permission, and as a radiant lamp."[6]

There is no escaping the need to turn to him and his manifest proof. One cannot go on ignoring his weight in guidance and knowledge, assuming that one can amass enough wisdom and information to guide his own path. Because no matter how excellent a man can become, one cannot do

---

[3] Al-Kulayni, *Al-Kafi*, 1:444 hadith 17. Narrating from Imam Ja'far Al-Sadiq.
[4] Al-Radi, *Nahjul Balagha*, 229.
[5] Ibid, 238.
[6] The Holy Quran, 33:45 – 46.

without the benefit that comes through the generosity of God's Messenger.

God certainly favored the faithful when He raised up among them an apostle from among themselves to recite to them His signs and to purify them and teach them the Book and wisdom, and earlier they had indeed been in manifest error.[7]

Indeed, the Prophet assumes a unique role as he brings together purification and education in his own person. With these two elements, he couples knowledge and action as they are the two veins in which the matters of life run through. One without the other would be a futile tool. For the Prophet's role in reform and development came in activating the willpower of the human being in bringing forth life in the things he would do. He actively participated in drawing out the road toward success and setting up the proper defense mechanisms in protecting that growth if any harm came its way. He said,

Do not anger God by pleasing any of his creation and do not seek closeness to any creation by distancing yourself from God the exalted. For there is nothing between God and any one of his creation that can give goodness or dispel evil except by His obedience and seeking His pleasure. Obedience to God is the success of every good that is sought and the salvation from every evil that is evaded. Surely, God protects those who obey Him, and those who disobey Him cannot find any protection against Him. The one who flees from

---

[7] The Holy Quran, 3:164.

God will see no refuge, for the will of God shall descend in his disgrace even if the creations detest it. And everything that shall come is near. What God wills is and what He does not will is not. 'Cooperate in piety and Godwariness, but do not cooperate in sin and aggression, and be wary of God. Indeed God is severe in retribution.' [8]

There is a narration that says, "One does not know what is with God, except by obeying Him..."[9] There are numerous calls, like this, for uprightness and following suit with wisdom and refraining from contradiction to the noble principles and values of the faith. In the end, it is to save oneself from harm or detriment that often cannot be fathomed.

A person of sound mind is called on to answer this call. After being warned from falling into vice, and acknowledging the risk of punishment involved, it would only be reasonable to heed to such warnings. It is in our nature to evade anything that is harmful or unfavorable to us, even if such harm is only possible and is not certain. Our reason dictates that we avoid going down a path of detriment and instead act in obedience to those calls, saving ourselves from damnation and suffering. This guidance is of course in need of a divine introduction to the creation, so that they may know their duty and their way towards salvation. Thus, God sent His messengers and prophets. As the Imam Ali (as) describes,

---

[8] Al-Sadouq, *Al-Amali*, 577. Citing: The Holy Quran, 5:2.
[9] Al-Beyhaqi, *Shu'b Al-Iman*, 7:299, II. 10376.

God chose prophets and took their pledge for his revelation and for carrying His message as their trust. In the course of time many people perverted God's trust with them and ignored His position and took compeers along with Him. Satan turned them away from knowing Him and kept them aloof from His worship. Then God sent His Messengers and series of His prophets towards them to get them to fulfil the pledges of His creation, to recall to them His bounties, to exhort them by preaching, to evoke in them the buried treasures of reason and show them the signs of His Omnipotence namely the sky which is raised over them, the earth that is placed beneath them, means of living that sustain them, deaths that overcome them, ailments that turn them old and incidents that successively betake them.

God never left His creation to remain without a Prophet deputized by Him, or a book sent down from Him or a binding argument or a standing plea. These Messengers were such that they did not feel little because of smallness of their number or of largeness of the number of their falsifiers. Among them was either a predecessor who would name the one to follow or the follower who had been introduced by the predecessor.

In this way ages passed by and times rolled on, fathers passed away while sons took their places till God deputized Muhammad (peace be upon him and his progeny) as His Prophet, in fulfilment of His promise and in completion of His Prophethood. His pledge had been taken from the Prophets, his traits of character were well reputed and his birth was honorable. The people of the earth at this time were divided in different parties, their aims were separate and ways were diverse. They either likened God with His creation or twisted His Names or turned to else than Him. Through Muhammad God guided them out of wrong and with his efforts took them out of ignorance.

Then God chose for Muhammad, peace be upon him [and on his progeny], to meet Him, selected him for His [own nearness], regarded him too dignified to remain in this world and decided to remove him from this place of trial. So He drew him towards Himself with honor. God may shower His blessing on him, and his progeny. The Prophet left among you the same which other Prophets left among their peoples, as Prophets do not leave [their people] untended without a clear path and a standing ensign...[10]

Sending the Holy Prophet was part of a divine mission to educate and develop a nation – one that had already had its own convictions and practices. If the messenger was not one who encompassed all the necessary traits to receive God's mercy and favor, and then distribute that message upon the rest of the nation, God would not have given him such a responsibility. If God would have assigned this task to someone who was not qualified it would have been an essential contradiction to the very mission itself. Moreover, God did not force the Prophet to have the qualifications he had; rather, it was a result of the Prophet's own free will. Otherwise, it would again go against the very point of the

---

[10] Al-Radi, *Nahjul Balagha*, Sermon 1.

system, to freely choose betterment, advancement, and excellence. If not for that freedom of choice, then we would not deserve the rewards for our deeds nor the punishments for our transgressions. If we were punished for something that we had no choice in doing, would that not be oppressive? Remember, "Your Lord does not wrong anyone.[11] Immaculate is He, and greatly exalted above what they say![12]"

Thus, the one who was sent – Prophet Muhammad – possessed the qualities and characteristics of excellence and readiness to inspire and rejuvenate the innate desire of the human being to strive for its own excellence and perfection. He understood well, and better than anyone else, the true meanings of success, virtue, and wisdom. That innate inclination towards excellence had to be nurtured and protected from the negative effects of society's customs that may not have had the same priorities in development and growth. Once a person leaves that path he will do an injustice to his own self. Because of this contradiction that sometimes existed between our natural pursuit and the swayed priorities of our societies, there had to be a guide to establish proof of God as a reminder of what is right and what is wrong. That proof was established and God's servants were on notice. With guidance they could now know for certain how to hold on to that natural desire built in all of us to excel and succeed.

---

[11] The Holy Quran, 18:49.
[12] The Holy Quran, 17:43.

The Messenger knew early on the importance of reforming our lives as human beings and advancing our human condition to what is better. He understood that such an undertaking would need to be comprehensive and consistent, because human beings are dynamic and complex. They are the subject matter of this reform; and such a system of development would need to suit and address the characteristics of the subject it wishes to advance. Such a platform of development would need to include several reform programs including the fundamental humbleness before the Creator, tolerance and coexistence with one's fellow human being, and a sense of duty and care to all other living things. With some of these essential components, your mindset and course of action will naturally become distant from vanity and violence. Instead, you will inherently become closer to virtue, wisdom, and even educating and mentoring others. This of course would depend on the individual's own capacity and energy. It also falls on their sense of responsibility in this regard and their acknowledgment of the great role played in such participation. The Holy Quran and the noble traditions of the Holy Prophet discuss this subject of virtuous reform, giving us a foundation to deepen our understanding of the root of human development, just as it serves as the one of the foundations of building our lives and realizing the roles we play.

Human development is not a new or modern subject. The subject was discussed and focused on after the end of World War II, especially with the defeated nations leaving their battlefields and going back home. It was not buildings and structures that were destroyed and destruction of material things that was so significant; rather, it was the shock left in the destruction of the human condition that was viewed as devastating. Accordingly, nations tried to quickly move themselves out of the environment of ruin and destruction, and figure how they could better their conditions. It is from this history that the term "human development" came about on a global level, and was primarily limited to discourse on economics and politics up until the 90s. The subject of human development did not crystalize in other intellectual discourse of human thought and epistemology until more recently.

However, this subject is deeply rooted in Islamic values and thought. It has its theoretical framework as well as its processes of implementation in the Holy Quran and the tradition of the Holy Prophet. The term human development has not always been used, even though the idea has been discussed and implemented for quite some time. This is because the pursuit for change, betterment, and growth is an intrinsic part of the human experience and a tool for the advancement of the human condition on Earth. It flows from our presence and being. Clarifying the notes and instructions of human development found in the heritage of Islam – both in the Holy Quran and in the prophetic tradition – and providing such clarity to the people is essential in this regard.

The Holy Prophet stressed the ability of man to develop himself for himself by himself, without leaving or isolating himself from his society. This concept alone connects all generations both in the past and the future, regardless of their geography or place in the world. God has given humanity a tremendous ability – cognitively and physically – in advancing its condition forward and providing for itself growth, maturity, and stability. Through its faculties, mankind is able to distinguish between what is beneficial and what is harmful, referring back to its values and understanding of the way the world works. In these assessments, a sense of responsibility and duty to others arises and the more one honors those duties the more growth will be realized.

People grow stronger when they work together, regardless of whether it is simple productivity or the designs of economics, politics, and financial systems. From this flows the dynamic functions of society and order, administration and authority, and the preservation and expansion of wealth. Establishing values of affinity to religion and nation, as well as preserving one's identity, and how this all plays within the idea of advancement and development of the human condition. These topics and others play a significant role in what humanity needs its experience and pursuit of excellence as it strives for its development, while it moves towards realizing the godly goal of rising to the position of viceroy.

Take a look at the following verses in the Quran,

"When your Lord said to the angels, 'Indeed I am going to set a viceroy on the earth,'"[13]

"'O David! Indeed, We have made you a vicegerent on the earth. So judge between people with justice,'"[14]

It is by God's promise that man is a dynamic subject of development, growth, and advancement of his society, entrusted with a duty that carries the greatest purpose.

"Indeed We presented the Trust to the heavens and the earth and the mountains, but they refused to undertake it and were apprehensive of it; but man undertook it."[15] Man has taken on such a responsibility which dictates that he is ready and capable for it, so long as he knows the rules of upholding this great trust and the expectations of a viceroy on earth.

---

[13] The Holy Quran, 2:30.
[14] The Holy Quran, 38:26.
[15] The Holy Quran, 33:72.

TEN PRINCIPLES FOR EXCELLENCE

In looking at the Holy Quran and its inspiration for human development, there are several principles that help guide us in reaching our individual and collective excellence. Such principles are supported by the examples of the Prophet and his disciples. Ten particular principles that stand out in this discourse are: purification, nurture, empowerment, harnessing potential, pursuit, good work, strategic planning, reform, integrity, and knowledge.

PURIFICATION

In the Holy Quran, there are verses that focus on the concept of human development and work within the general idea of such development. Take the example of purification when God says, "By the soul and Him who fashioned it, and inspired it with [discernment between] its virtues and vices: one who purifies it is felicitous, and one who betrays it fails."[1]

Purification here is a reference to growth, betterment, and refining oneself. These are some of the essential goals of human development and are necessary components to it. They are used to fight corruption; without purification, human values would simply disappear.

NURTURE

Nurture and development have a significant relationship. God says in the Holy Quran, "He brought you forth from the earth and made it your habitation. So plead with Him for forgiveness, then turn to Him penitently. My Lord is indeed very near [and] responsive.'"[2] These two elements are significant in their relation to the human beings' ability to advance in their existence – to the extent of their will and effort.

Our potential to grow and advance is not met simply by what we have structurally in our natural physical being. Nurture plays a huge role in growing the competency we have to develop and harness the potential we have as individuals.

Through thought and faith, the innate will to succeed and grow is reinforced. The nurture provided by thought and belief serves as a fundamental component to the effectiveness of one's path to development. Otherwise, there would

---

[1] The Holy Quran, 91:10.
[2] The Holy Quran, 11:61.

be no feasibility to human development programs without the proper qualifications or competency to accomplish the goals they set out to achieve.

EMPOWERMENT

God says, "Certainly We have established you on the earth, and made in it [various] means of livelihood for you."[3] God has empowered us with the tools and ways to seek our self-improvement and development. This notion of establishment is all encompassing, we have the means to succeed and flourish in our lives. At the same time, acknowledging and utilizing these means is what many human development programs continue to lack. The tools are before us, we merely have to reflect on that reality and acknowledge it. Once we do that, we are intrinsically empowered to conquer any obstacle we face.

HARNESSING

There is a beautiful verse on potential and what God has given us of blessings in the Holy Quran,

> *Do you not see that God has disposed for you whatever there is in the heavens and whatever there is in the earth and He has showered upon you His blessings, the outward, and the inward?*[4]

---

[3] The Holy Quran, 7:10.
[4] The Holy Quran, 31:20.

God has harnessed all the resources and tools in the world at the disposal of man. It is up to us to benefit from all that is between the heavens and Earth, for God has made it for us – for our advancement, for our excellence. He says "Who made the earth tractable for you; so walk on its flanks and eat of His provision, and towards Him is the resurrection."[5] If man is to misuse, at times, the bounties and natural resources that God has bestowed us with then there is a natural reaction to such decadence.

Corruption has appeared in land and sea because of the doings of the people's hands, that He may make them taste something of what they have done, so that they may come back.[6]

Those natural resources are threatened, at times, by the natural disasters that result or plague-like epidemics that take place. In such crises, people are naturally inclined, or even forced, to return to their senses, wisdom, and better use of their means and resources. Continual human development and growth is realized, even in imperfect circumstances.

PURSUIT

The Holy Quran speaks of the pursuit of man, beautifully summarizing "That nothing belongs to man except what he strives for."[7] It reflects the reality that we must rely on ourselves to realize our goals and aspirations in life. Further-

---

[5] The Holy Quran, 67:15.
[6] The Holy Quran, 30:41.
[7] The Holy Quran, 53:39.

more, we must own up to the responsibility of what we have accomplished and carry on in our journey of pursuit without shortchanging the pursuit or settling. Striving in life encompasses the start of the journey towards one's goals, enhancing what we already have of experience, talent or potential, and renewing or revamping our tools of execution.

It includes innovating new methods, finding creative means, and doing whatever is necessary in putting forth our full efforts to advance ourselves as individuals that will in turn develop our communities as a whole. It is the idea of striving and pursuit that entices us to take on responsibility, individual and common, and makes it a priority of both the citizen and the state. So long as pursuit for betterment exists, the sense of responsibility is not forgotten. The Holy Prophet says,

> *Every one of you is a shepherd and every one of you is responsible [for his flock]. The leader of people is a guardian and is responsible for his subjects. A man is the guardian of his family and he is responsible for them. A woman is the guardian of her husband's home and she is responsible for them. The servant is a guardian of the property of his master and he is responsible for it. No doubt, every one of you is a shepherd and is responsible [for his flock].[8]*

The Holy Prophet also said,

> *The feet of no man will move on the Day of Judgment until he is asked of four: about his age and how he expended it,*

---

[8] Ahmad ibn Hanbal, *Musnad Ahmad*, 2:5; Al-'Ahsa'i, *'Awali Al-La'ali*, 1:129.

his youth and how he spent it, his money and how he gained it and spent it, and his love for us Ahlulbayt.[9]

GOOD WORK

Putting forth hard work and effort in any endeavor is instrumental to the success of that objective for several reasons. God says,

Say, 'Go on working: God will see your conduct, and His Apostle and the faithful [as well], and you will be returned to the Knower of the sensible and the Unseen, and He will inform you concerning what you used to do.[10]

Emphasizing the importance of work and effort, God promises that "As for those who have faith and do righteous deeds—indeed We do not waste the reward of those who are good in deeds."[11] The promise here of reward and not taking any deeds for granted reinforces us to work harder in general, and more specifically on enhancing our resources for growth and development. We are being guaranteed that our work and effort will not go in vain, that we are accountable for what we do and will be rewarded accordingly. Acknowledging this has a natural effect on us and entices us to genuinely exert our efforts with the hopes of achieving success or at least to avoid failure.

---

9 Al-Sadouq, *Al-Amali*, 93, I I. 73.
10 The Holy Quran, 9:105.
11 The Holy Quran, 18:30.

Whether this work is in worship or professional practice, physical or spiritual, it pushes people forward to reach their goals – whether it is out of fear of failure or ambition. Thus, it preserves the continuity of growth, in the diverse fields of work and progress, and the world continues to be built up.

The Holy Prophet emphasized this himself. He said, "God did not send any prophet except as a shepherd of flock." His companions asked, "And you O Messenger of God?" He answered, "And I used to take care of the people of Mecca through weights and scale."[12] In the same light, "The Holy Prophet purchased caravans from the Levant, to which he used from it to pay off his debts and distribute the rest amongst his relatives…"[13]

Khadija bint Khuwaylid was one of the first woman merchants in Arabia. She was known for her honor and tremendous success in business. She would hire men to sell the products of her business and compensate them based on commission, incentivizing their sales. When she was informed about the Messenger of God and his high moral character, ethics and noble traits, she had a message sent to him. She offered for him to be her agent in Greater Syria, promising him better compensation than any of the other merchants that worked in her enterprise. She also would have one of her young assistants, his name was Maysara, accompany the Prophet in his travels. The Holy Prophet accepted her offer and set out to Syria with Maysara. The

---

[12] Ibn Majja, *Al-Sunnan*, 2:727; Ibn Sa'ad, *Al-Tabaqat*, 1:125.
[13] Al-Kulayni, *Al-Kafi*, 5:75, H. 8.

Prophet sold the products that he carried and then purchased some other goods from the area. He then returned to Mecca with a caravan heading in that direction. When he arrived in Mecca, he brought the goods he purchased back to Khadija. She was able to double her profit upon her sale of those goods.[14]

The Prophet taught us that hands on work was of great benefit to us. From farming and agriculture to trade and craftsmanship, he encouraged the type of practical work that involved one's active participation in the physical sense. "There is no sweeter gain than what is earned by one's own toil,"[15] the Prophet said. He didn't stop there though. The Prophet stressed the quality of one's work and that people consciously put their best efforts forward in their professions, creating a higher sense of work ethic within the fabric of Muslim thought.

He said, "God loves that if any of you are going to work [on something] that he perfect it."[16] Similar to what was narrated previously about the gains of one's work, the Prophet relates that to a person's effort and quality of work. There is a direct relationship between one's gains or income resulting from work and the quality of their work ethic. "The best of gains are the gains of a worker who excels in his work."[17]

---

[14] Ibn Ishaaq, *Al-Sira*, 60, ll. 58.

[15] Ibn Majja, *Al-Sunnan*, 2:724, ll. 2138.

[16] Al-Mosuli, *Musnad Abi Ya'la*, 7:350, ll. 4386; Al-Tabarani, *Al-Mu'jam Al-Awsat*, 1:275. See also: Al-Haythami, *Majma' Al-Zawa'id*, 4:98.

[17] Ahmad ibn Hanbal, *Musnad Ahmad*, 2:334.

As it was not in the Prophet's character to merely advise people on how to lead their lives in virtue, he consistently practiced what he preached and set the higher example. When it came to caring for the burial rites of fellow Muslims, the Prophet would bury fallen believers with his own hands. He carried the body of Saad ibn Ma'ath down to his grave. He would tell the people near him, "Hand me a rock and give me some moist soil." He poured the soil of the ground over his body and place the slab of stone over it. He performed all the rituals and did them to best possible degree. After he finished he then said, "I know that this grave will be worn down [with time] but God loves a servant that if he does something, he does it well."[18]

This narration shows us how serious the Prophet was in practicing what he advised, using some of the most psychologically sensitive situations such as death to effectively reach people's senses and correct what many had belittled or taken for granted.

Through his example he could redirect people to pay closer attention to those things that would have such a negative impact on their lives. It would bring light to different forms of waste of corruption, be it administrative, professional, or financial. Waste and corruption are definitely destructive to people, on an individual basis, and as societies and countries at large. If these defects and negative tendencies are not addressed early on through human development efforts, no

---

[18] Al-Amili, *Wasa'il Al-Shia*, 2:884; Citing: Al-Sadouq, Al-Amali, 468.

matter how much planning is put forth, countries will face an even greater challenge in warding off these different forms of corruption. That would in turn go to undermine human development programs and functions.

STRATEGIC PLANNING

To properly prepare and plan for development programs and future projects and ideas, it is essential for the actualization of such projects. The fact is that development is dependent on strategy, studying both the individual and collective situation of the community, and providing an assessment of the pros and cons that exist. After analyzing the state of individuals and communities, it is appropriate to provide tailored solutions that address the current challenges, and then offer reasonable projections based on incorporating those solutions or neglecting them. It is as God said in the Holy Quran to the believers when they were being attacked,

> *Prepare against them whatever you can of [military] power and war-horses, awing thereby the enemy of God, and your enemy, and others besides them, whom you do not know, but God knows them. And whatever you spend in the way of God will be repaid to you in full, and you will not be wronged.[19]*

It should not take away from the subject that this verse was in a military context; instead, we take from the parallel that

---

[19] The Holy Quran, 8:60.

war offers as immediate challenges to a community. Given that war is a temporary emergency, it still requires planning. In fact, planning is even more essential if one wishes the war to be as short-lived as possible. In addressing all the emergencies and challenges we face in life, planning is a fundamental tool to help overcome them with greater ease.

Take the example of Prophet Joseph when he advised the people, "You will sow for seven consecutive years. Then leave in the ear whatever [grain] you harvest, except a little that you eat."[20] He showed how important it was to plan for the future. From this and other prophetic experiences we can realize the significance of strategic planning, think tanks, and other projects and institutions designed to study the past and present as well as plan for the future. Ensuring food and shelter are naturally essential for the livelihood of any community; however, beyond that comes the more complex necessities of life that require planning and longer term thinking as well. It is this forward thinking approach that ensures the growth and development of our communities, and humanity at large. In order to serve the advancement of humanity we must work and plan for it. Such an approach follows suit with the prophetic saying, "The best of people are those who help people."[21]

---

[20] The Holy Quran, 12:47.
[21] Al-Beyhaqi, *Shu'b Al-Iman*, 6:117, H. 7658.

INTEGRITY

God says, "So be steadfast, just as you have been commanded—[you] and whoever has turned [to God] with you—and do not overstep the bounds. Indeed, He watches what you do."[22] Steadfastness or integrity is insurance for our consistency in our work and daily dealings. Realizing that we have to do what is right, regardless of the time or situation, builds a consistency in our character that is part to our overall development as ethical human beings. It is what holds us back from betraying our faith, our families, and our own selves. It is what allows us to be trusted because our character is at a level that when we are entrusted with anything, be it a prized possession or a personal secret, we honor it as if it is our own. That is why the Holy Prophet said, "There is no faith for one who cannot be trusted."[23]

The Prophet also described trust by saying,

> *Whoever dishonors a trust in this world and did not return it to its owners before his death has died on a path other than mine. And he will meet God while God is angry with him.*[24]

These narrations clearly show us the extent by which believers should distance themselves from obtaining these negative traits. If a person cannot be trusted, he removes himself from the status of being a believer. He brings upon himself

---

[22] The Holy Quran, 11:112.
[23] Ahmad ibn Hanbal, *Musnad Ahmad*, 3:135.
[24] Al-Sadouq, *Al-Amali*, 5:133, H. 7.

the wrath of God and moves farther away from what is characteristic of being a Muslim. Poverty, both literal and figurative, is closer to a person who has betrayed the trust of his family, friends, and colleagues. Of course, if one is aware of these negativities he would want to stay as far away from them as possible.

On that note, the Holy Prophet would emphasize the importance of looking at one's behavior not for individual or personal acts but the things that involve engagement with others as well. He said,

> Do not look at how much they pray or fast, how many times they go on pilgrimage... or how long they prolong their worship at night; rather, look at truthfulness in speech and fulfillment of trusts.[25]

It is not enough to have personal conviction in rituals and worship, one's conviction must be translated in action that is reflection in our relationships within the community. There is a big difference between those who implement their faith through their consistency and trustworthiness with others and those who merely practice specific rituals that are individual or personal in nature. Of course, both practices are necessary and important. Thus, true development in faith and practice requires both. God describes the believers in the Holy Quran,

> Certainly, the faithful have attained salvation —those who are humble in their prayers, avoid vain talk, carry out their

---

[25] Ibid, 379, 11. 6.

[duty of] zakat, guard their private parts, (except from their spouses or their slave women, for then they are not blameworthy; but whoever seeks [anything] beyond that—it is they who are transgressors), and those who keep their trusts and covenants and are watchful of their prayers. It is they who will be the inheritors, who shall inherit paradise and will remain in it [forever].[26]

These verses praise the believers for their steadfastness as individuals, their spiritual commitment, and their consistency in that. He also praises them for their commitment on the community level, in fulfilling their trusts and promises. In manifesting all of these traits, a believer's natural reward is paradise. He who makes it his priority to follow through spiritually, intellectually, physically, and financially in his commitment to both individual and community responsibilities will have this excellent result.

REFORM

When an individual works to rid himself of deficiencies or impurities, he consequently affects the overall state of the community's own deficiencies as well. As individuals work on themselves, they have an impact on the collective. It is a form of purification or refinement that is needed as a prerequisite to development and advancement. When Prophet Shu'ayb spoke to his people he said,

---

[26] The Holy Quran, 23:1 – 11.

O my people! Have you considered, should I stand on a manifest proof from my Lord, who has provided me a good provision from Himself? I do not wish to oppose you by what I forbid you. I only desire to put things in order, as far as I can, and my success lies only with God: in Him I have put my trust, and to Him I turn penitently.[27]

His response to his people stressed the role of the individual within a society. The individual plays a fundamental role in societal reform. If reform does not take place on an individual level, the whole discussion on human development becomes more abstract and theoretical than practical. There is a need to acknowledge the role each individual plays within society. Every person plays a part in community advancement and every individual counts. This is not something to belittle or take for granted.

KNOWLEDGE

Gaining knowledge is a prerequisite to personal development. It allows a person to respond to opportunities of advancement and growing as an individual. With knowledge, the values and principles necessary for one's progress and growth are easier to realize and implement. God says in the Holy Quran, "Say, 'Are those who know equal to those who do not know?' Only those who possess intellect take admonition."[28]

---

[27] The Holy Quran, 11:88.
[28] The Holy Quran, 39:9.

Many people practically neglect this fundamental truth, that knowledge is so very important and necessary for the overall success and growth of the individual. When God refers to "those of intellect" in the Holy Quran it is clear what significance knowledge holds in the status of the human being with God. It is seen often in the Holy Quran how God distinguishes between people based on their knowledge, as knowledge often relates to a person's virtue and ethics or at the very least the potential they have in virtue and excellence. God says,

> *It is He who made the sun a radiance and the moon a light, and ordained its phases that you might know the number of years and the calculation [of time]. God did not create all that except with justice. He elaborates the signs for a people who have knowledge.*[29]

These ten fundamental principles are supported by the teachings of the Holy Quran and the prophetic tradition. The value in man is great and Islam makes it a priority to provide for humanity's comprehensive intellectual, physical, and personal development. Faith desires that we grow with a commitment to these values and principles of truth, so that each individual is able to succeed for himself and contribute back to his society. Being God's most precious and prized creation, human beings encompass the ideals of love and brotherhood, chivalry and bravery, and reform and success. The Holy Prophet worked to establish these values by

---

[29] The Holy Quran, 10:5.

making clear for his followers what their sources of guidance should be — God's Book and the Holy Household. Through those tools, people could achieve their potential and attain success.

The Holy Prophet's choice in human development came with what showed within himself of hard work and perseverance. He showed his deep care those around him, in that he wanted them to be successful and to attain what was better for themselves. He was ambitious in that regard, helping others grow, develop and advance. His character and example provided the first steps for community and societal reform, as the change and development of a community could only come from within before expanding outward.

Very early on, the Prophet made it a priority to establish a cohesive system of thought and ethics. The task of that system would be to start the fundamental reform that was needed to provide for human development in society. The system would be embedded with universal humanitarian values and principles. It called on its community with a spirit of brotherhood and love. It abhorred taking advantage of one another or taking each other for granted. No longer would special interests, personal interests, or any interests that sacrificed the wellbeing of others, take precedence over our principles and values. Individuals were not merely units or numbers, they were persons with rights and obligations that brought value to society. Knowing the impact of the environment on individuals, and not wanting his followers to be unequipped to meet the challenges they will face, he would strive to establish this system as a way to guard themselves from impediments and pursue their development.

The Prophet saw the problems people faced. He lived with his people and felt their pain. He knew their problems and challenges. He was a man of the people with unmatched empathy and proven participative leadership. As a leader and a prophet, his mission was simple – to provide the best system of ethics for the people. While others were busy with pursuing their personal interests, through blackmail and extortion, the Prophet remained as the exemplary visionary that would lead his nation through his service in ethics and virtue. The human condition does not forget nor can it ignore the negative experiences of violence, war, and corruption that it has gone through. Human beings can do terrible things indeed; however, they can do the greatest things as well.

There is a real need for the continuous guidance of the selected few who are empowered by God to guide humanity from the darkness they may fall into back to the light. That is why God says, "Take whatever the Apostle gives you, and refrain from whatever he forbids you, and be wary of God. Indeed God is severe in retribution."[30] It is a clear and necessary directive to be aligned with what the Prophet provides us. Otherwise, it would be a deviation from not only what God desires for us, but from attaining our own success and reaching our potential in our development.

---

[30] The Holy Quran, 59:7.

From some of the most fundamental principles that the Prophet brought forth is strengthening the ties between individuals and crystalizing the values of love and brotherhood between people's souls. This principle is by far one of the most important principles of life. It is narrated that the Prophet said, "The best of people are those who benefit people."[31] The prophetic approach to life and community is one of collaboration, cooperation, and teamwork.

> *A Muslim is a brother to his fellow Muslim. He does not oppress him nor does he give him up. Whoever is there for his brother in need, God will be there for him during his need. And whoever relieves a Muslim of a plight, God will relieve him of one his plights on the Day of Judgment. And whoever [does not expose] a Muslim [of his faults], God will [not expose him] on the Day of Judgment.[32]*

Whoever adopts Islam and made it his way of life then they will naturally follow its prophet. In doing so that person encompasses himself within the love and grace of God. Speaking of God's love the Prophet would tell the Muslims as instructed in the Quran, "Follow me and God will love you and forgive you your sins."[33] Though that we see the formation of a triangle of faith between God, the messenger, and those receiving the message. In this relationship, there were two dimensions to human development.

---

[31] Al-Beyhaqi, *Shu'b Al-Iman*, 6:117, hadith 7658

[32] Ahmad ibn Hanbal, *Musnad Ahmad*, 2:91.

[33] The Holy Quran, 3:31.

The first of the two dimensions is human development in all its different levels or aspects. For development goes to enhance a person's capabilities and potential spiritually, intellectually, psychologically, physically, and socially. Through that the person will face the changes that take place in his life, especially as he looks deep into his position and reflects on his status. Realizing that development comes on all these levels, one can maximize on the talents that they have and work on their weaknesses depending on the particular area of development.

The second dimension is utilizing the resources that exist within a community to allow for maximum growth and development for people. It is essential to acknowledge what exists of technology, methods, and resources and use them with the greatest utility for the greatest benefit. The understanding of "the best of people are those who benefit people," is essentially working along these two dimensions simultaneously. Whereby we work on the growth of people and empowering their creativity in development, without compromising their spiritual and ethical principles by advancing their material or physical state. It is creating that balance between the two that allows for wholesome and comprehensive growth. We are in need of both spiritual and intellectual development, as well as social, financial, and material growth.

Given that man is the viceroy of God on Earth, the role that man plays and the importance given to his development is immense. We cannot only look at one aspect or dimension of his existence, and consequently his growth. Our approach must be comprehensive, as we are made of soul and body. It is these two that make us the human beings who we are. Acknowledging this and working on this bases allows to reach the "paradise as vast as the heavens and the earth, prepared for the Godwary."[34]

Remember, "The life of this world is nothing but diversion and play, but the abode of the Hereafter is indeed Life (itself), had they known!"[35] Those of intellect will not compromise what is everlasting for something that is finite. We have to make sure that our ambitions and pursuits fall within this understanding; otherwise, much of what we do may go in vain. Money, power, and influence may be ambitions that we think will bring us the success and status that we want for ourselves. However, if it is not within the framework we have outlined and the principles established that bring that balance for mind, body, and spirit, it will likely bring us only ruin in the end.

---

[34] The Holy Quran, 3:133.
[35] The Holy Quran, 29:64.

COMPASSION FOR CHANGE

THE MECHANISM FOR REFORM

Compassion is one of the most fundamental human traits within a society. It is the element that fills the much of the void that can exist between human beings on a psychological and spiritual level. Having compassion for one another brings ease, tranquility, and stability within families, communities and societies at large. There is a desire in every human being to be loved and dealt with through empathy and compassion. Humanity, unfortunately, has experienced the opposite of this in one way or another.

Violence, selfishness, hate, and harshness take over many people's lives. One act leads to another, habits are formed, and a culture is made. Islam was against these behaviors in its plan for human development. There is no room for hate and violence in faith. Instead, love and compassion are the virtues that are ultimately promoted and implemented in pursuit of human development. Individuals are encouraged to bond and work with another to advance each other. No one should feel like an outcast, left out, or estranged.

In line with this principle, there are a number of narrations from the Holy Prophet regarding the significance of compassion. It is the best tool to have in securing real peaceful coexistence within a society. Compassion allows us to acknowledge our differences as potential strengths and even celebrate them. It empowers us to work together within the domain of our many commonalities and further our relationships to build our communities. Compassion guarantees that we forgive each other and not allow misunderstandings get in the way of our work as a community.

Take a look at the following narrations on the subject of compassion, all from the Holy Prophet.

"As for the compassionate ones, the Most Compassionate will show them compassion. Have compassion for those on Earth, those in the Heavens will have compassion for you..."[1]

"God has compassion for his compassionate servants."[2]

"Whoever does not have compassion for people, God will not have compassion for him."[3]

"Whoever does not have compassion, will not be dealt with compassion. Whoever does not forgive, will not be forgiv-

---

[1] Al-Tirmidhi, *Sunan Al-Tirmidhi*, 3:217, 11. 1989.

[2] Ahmad ibn Hanbal, *Musnad Ahmad*, 5:204.

[3] Ibid, 4:385.

en. Whoever does not accept repentance, his repentance will not be accepted."[4]

"Whoever is compassionate, even if it is with a bird to be slaughtered, God will show him compassion on the Day of Judgment."[5]

Someone told the Prophet, "I would love for my Lord to forgive me." The Prophet replied, "Forgive yourself and show compassion to God's creation, God will forgive you."[6]

"A caller from hellfire calls out, 'O Kind, O Beneficent, rescue me from hellfire!' God orders an angel to remove the caller and bring him before God. He will ask the caller, 'Did you even show compassion to a bird?'"[7]

"Whoever does not show compassion to those on Earth, he will not be shown compassion by those in the Heavens."[8]

"By the One that my soul is in His hands, no one but the compassionate will enter Heaven." Some of the individuals around him replied, "We are all compassionate." He said, "No, [you are not] until you show compassion to all."[9]

"You do not believe until you love. Would you like to know how you should love each other?" They said, "Yes, O Messenger of God." He said, "Spread peace amongst yourselves and [there will be] love. By the One that my soul is in His

---

[4] Al-Tabarani, *Al-Mu'jam Al-Kabeer*, 2:351.

[5] Ibid, 8:234.

[6] Al-Muttaqqi Al-Hindi, *Kanz Al-Ummal*, 16:128.

[7] Ibid, 3:167, II. 5992.

[8] Al-Tabarani, *Al-Mu'jam Al-Kabeer*, 2:355.

[9] Al-Muttaqqi Al-Hindi, *Kanz Al-Ummal*, 3:167, II. 5989.

hands, you will not enter Heaven until you are compassionate." They said, "O Messenger of God, we are all compassionate." He replied, "It is not by merely being compassionate to one another, it is compassion with all, compassion with all."[10]

"None of you will enter Heaven except those who are compassionate." They replied, "O Messenger of God, we are all compassionate." He said, "Not the compassion that you have for yourselves or your families, it is until you have compassion for the people."[11]

"God is compassionate and loves the compassionate ones. He shows his compassion to all those that are compassionate."[12]

"Disenchanted and failed is the servant whom God did not place in his heart compassion for people."[13]

In one particular narration he speaks directly to Imam Ali on this subject saying,

> O Ali, seek good from the compassionate ones within my nation and you will live in their care. Do not seek good from those of hardened hearts, for damnation is upon them. O Ali, God has created what is good and created for it its people. He made what is good loved by them and made them love doing what is good. He directed its seekers to them just like water is directed through dry earth so that the earth and

---

10 Al-Hakim Al-Nisabouri, *Al-Mustadrak*, 4:168.
11 Al-Beyhaqi, *Shu'b Al-Iman*, 7:479, H. 11059.
12 Al-Muttaqqi Al-Hindi, *Kanz Al-Ummal*, 4:249, H. 10381.
13 Al-Siyouti, *Al-Jami' Al-Sagheer*, 1:598, H. 3873.

its people may live through it. O Ali, the people of good in this world are the people of good in the hereafter.[14]

The Prophet's directives in these numerous narrations show how he stressed on having an environment of care, love, and compassion amongst people. People ought to be empathetic towards one another, and not simply their family and friends. That way the community protects itself and no one would feel deprived or in need if we all looked out for one another, be it financially and materially or emotionally and psychologically. Power, authority, and money cannot buy you the comfort and care that comes with genuine community relationships. Believers must be there for each other and must shine as that example for those who are near and far. The Messenger of God said, "Indeed the believer finds refuge in another believer just like one who is thirsty finds a haven in cool water."[15]

This spiritual and moral connection that the Prophet promoted is integral to the system of human development. It was inclusive of parts of the human experience that most had neglected, and continue to neglect, as necessary for wholesome growth. The Prophet came to his people in his role as a spiritual guide, a teacher of ethics, and a father for all. Describing his divine mission he said, "I was sent to perfect the best of ethics."[16] That very statement reaffirms the natural tendency we have as human beings towards ethical

---

14 Al-Hakim Al-Nisabouri, *Al-Mustadrak*, 4:321.

15 Al-Rawandi, *Al-Nawadir*, 100.

16 Al-Beyhaqi, *Al-Sunan Al-Kubra*, 10:192.

conduct. We were created with the tools to behave ethically and the Prophet came to sharpen the saw in our toolbox and polish and shine every other tool we have for the matter.

Though intrinsically we are bound for ethics, we are still in need of that guide to keep us on task. The guide is there to remind us and gently pull us back on course when we lose our way. He sets the example and is there for us to emulate. He does not merely tell us the way, he shows it to us. God told the Prophet, "Indeed you possess a great character."[17] He described him in another verse speaking to the believers as "a mercy for those of you who have faith."[18]

God told the people about the Holy Prophet Muhammad, "There has certainly come to you an apostle from among yourselves. Grievous to him is your distress; he has deep concern for you, and is most kind and merciful to the faithful."[19] Finally, in speaking to the Holy Prophet himself God clearly states the purpose for which he was sent. "We did not send you but as a mercy to all the nations."[20]

THE PROPHET'S EXAMPLE

The Prophet was that excellent example for people to follow and emulate in all godly virtues. "There is certainly a good exemplar for you in the Apostle of God—for those

---

[17] The Holy Quran, 68:4.
[18] The Holy Quran, 9:61.
[19] The Holy Quran, 9:128.
[20] The Holy Quran, 21:107.

who look forward to God and the Last Day, and remember God much."[21]

Thus, there is no surprise that Muslims are deeply influenced by the story of his life. It is from his life that we implant the values and principles of faith in ourselves as individuals. From that, we are able to spread it as a collective within our communities and society. It starts from individual persons that desire to follow his excellent example. That becomes a community of virtue and ethics. When we follow that example, we are able to properly represent the faith of Islam wherever we may be. Whether it is in our nations or in foreign countries, it is this example that connects us to our Creator and the rest of creation.

At the forefront of all the principles we have discussed is compassion. The Prophet would show how important it was to lead a life of compassion, providing an alternative narrative to what many had chosen in life of darkness and ignorance.

Compassion, he would show, would triumph over violence and hate. That triumph could come through every level of society if people were to believe and practice it. Through compassion people could forgive, work together, and accept one another for who they were. All of those desired effects are an extension of compassion. In fact, they are from the attributes of God of which He placed the desire in the hearts of His servants to emulate.

---

[21] The Holy Quran, 33:21.

Forgiveness, tolerance, and compassion are things that God embedded in our hearts. Be it with family members or friends and colleagues, young or old, male or female, rich or poor, Muslim or not, compassion should be the forte of our dealings. Compassion, as taught by the Holy Prophet, extends to all living things – animals and plants alike. When this prophetic way of life is implemented, society will see its positive impact. Such an impact would rightly render the members of our society to be filled with pride and honor.

Human development is a process of advancing one's capabilities and enhancing the utilization of talents in the different areas and functions of life. Such a process is used to promote positive change and reform in society, which will help strengthen and grow the society at large. Human development can also be seen as a self-correcting process of coming to what is better over a period of time in different places in the world. Compassion aides this process and helps its realization between individuals. It is not limited to a few people, because as it spreads in action it becomes embedded in the psyche of society. With compassionate thinking people feel the responsibility towards reform and positive change, not merely for themselves but for others. Nonetheless, change begins on an individual basis. Personal participation in this process has a tremendous role in reform and advancement, as the responsibility for such reform is one shared by all. If each individual carries out this personal responsibility, it will have a domino effect which results in real change on a community level. There is no need to coercively change those around us, we must simply work on changing ourselves. Once each individual does that we are inadvertently helping one another change and form a society based on compassion, virtue, and ethics.

The Holy Prophet's style of human development uniquely relies on the individual as a mechanism for its success. For the individual is changing by himself, for himself, with an inadvertent impact on others. The individual creates change through care and empathy, feeling the value of what he sets forth, and thus does not neglect it. Many other forms or styles of human development have relied on government and policy centers. Naturally, such reliance comes with the reality that these centers push certain agendas that benefit particular groups or individuals. It lacks the grassroots power found in individual-based development. People are not empowered as individual catalysts of change. Individuals may be weakened before these greater mechanisms or institutions and give up before they are able to accomplish anything for themselves. This is what the Prophet wanted to avoid.

Instead, he made the individual the centerpiece of his vision for human development. He began with the individual so that the end result can be for the individual. The human being became focus of this dynamic discussion, whereby programs and processes of development and reform are centered around the individual not the other way around. Development and reform must be tailored for communities and nations. These programs should be flexible and adapt depending on the people it is serving. This was what the Prophet wanted.

Other styles of development, however, did not have the same notion in this regard. Their idea of success came from the strict implementation of policies from government – top to bottom. They looked at people as mere recipients without a real role to be played in development. They are to receive the policy or plan as a collective. The individual does not play a significant part as an individual. God says in the Holy Quran that He will not change what is within a nation until they change what is within themselves. His promise for change comes with that active pursuit for reform by individuals. Each individual is an actor himself and not merely a tool to be used by others in their vision of change.

Of course, the notion of compassion is not something that will be seen throughout society as it is a choice to be made by one's free will. It is contingent, like other actions of free will, on a person's real willingness to reform. Otherwise, no one can be forced to show compassion in pursuit of betterment and development. "So that he who perishes might perish by a manifest proof, and he who lives may live on by a manifest proof,"[22] God says in the Holy Quran.

It is through free will, through that choice that is allotted to every human being, by which he is accountable and will answer to. If we use our free will in making that better choice, the choice of compassion, we will surely fair as best in our

---

[22] The Holy Quran, 8:42.

outcomes – both in this life and the next. Each individual is responsible for his decisions. We carve our own paths. We are responsible, because we are able. That ability allows us to choose compassion, a choice that serves as a foregrounds for true comprehensive collective growth.

In the end, compassion is not merely for the benefit of the individual choosing it, it naturally encompasses everyone giving or receiving it. Its impact continues to permeate and reignite the tools and mechanisms for growth and development so long as it is activated. Through compassion we rise as human beings. We rise above oppressing others and stripping people of their rights. We rise above hurting one another and employing violence or hate as tools for control and influence. Individuals are enfranchised and communities are actually built. Through compassion, we begin the change within.

JUSTICE FOR LEADERSHIP

THE JUSTICE OF ALI IBN ABI TALIB

The ideas of development and leadership come together, naturally, as we aim to grow and lead ourselves from what is good to what is better. Leadership encompasses ourselves and others. To be an effective leader of oneself and others, the concept of justice cannot be neglected.

Imam Ali ibn Abi Talib worked diligently to establish justice both during his tenure as caliph and well before it. The Commander of the Faithful had a particular principle that he held near and dear. It was to preserve people's rights and make those who governed accountable to their citizens. Society was not to be left for the wolves and coldhearted, people had to be protected and honored. He emphasized the significance of this principle as well as the notion that human life cannot be taken for granted. He made a clear promise to uphold this principle.

*By God, I will take revenge for the oppressed from the op-
pressor and will pull the oppressor by the nose [like a reined
camel] and drag him to the spring of truthfulness even
though he may grudge it.[1]*

The Imam established justice amongst the people and
showed them its practical application. He attempted to impart it in people so it can become part of who they are and
translate into their dealings as a community. He showed that
justice is not merely wanted in theory but actually desired in
society, as it can lead to security, economic prosperity, and
general peace. That just governance brought by Imam Ali's
leadership provided individuals with contentment in their
affairs as they saw the rights of the collective being ad-
vanced. The Commander of the Faithful was asked, which
of the two is better; justice or generosity? He replied,

*Justice puts things in their places while generosity takes them
out from their directions; justice is the general caretaker
while generosity is a particular benefit. Consequently, justice
is superior and more distinguished of the two.[2]*

The Imam also said "There is a wide scope in dispensation
of justice, and he who finds it hard to act justly will find it
harder to deal with injustice."[3] He made it clear that justice
ensures the permanence of dignified living against oppression, aggression, and suppression. In fact, justice allows for
peace to perpetuate and for people to fulfill their ambitions

---

[1] Al-Radhi, *Nahj Al-Balagha*, 2:19, Letter 136.

[2] Ibid, 4:102, Tradition 437.

[3] Ibid, 1:45, Sermon 15.

and aspirations without violating the rights of others. Thus, a major part of Imam Ali's plan for reform was establishing equality and fairness, eradicating social classes, eliminating privileges gained through nepotism and affiliation, and instituting true equity for all so the entire society can be encompassed by structural justice.

The Imam did not only preach these principles and implement it by his own person, he managed to channel it through his senior appointees and governors. He provided them with specific instructions on upholding justice and fairness and not neglecting the rights of their citizens. In appointing Malik Al-Ashtar as his new governor in Egypt he directed him the following.

> *Habituate your heart to mercy for the subjects and to affection and kindness for them. Do not stand over them like greedy beasts who feel it is enough to devour them, since they are of two kinds, either your brother in religion or one like you in creation.*[4]

Justice came through compassion. The Imam aimed to establish justice with compassion and eliminate any form of authoritarian abuse. He set the standard for just governance that governors were to be measured against. It was a standard of accountability for the people with their rulers and the rulers with their people. Authorities were not to use their power to usurp people's rights or control the wealth of the people in the name of preserving the rule of law. A gover-

---

[4] Ibid, 3:84, Letter 53.

nor is appointed to take care of his constituents and safe-guard their rights. If that is not upheld, then the underlying purpose of governorship is defeated.

Moreover, tribalism and class affiliation was consciously set aside. Imam Ali taught us that the shared commonalities be-tween people supersede the differences they may have. People were to embrace these commonalities and leverage them to advance the common good, as an essential tool of social justice. This helps immensely in fostering stability and security in a society, especially one that suffers from a gov-ernment that does not govern based on principle. Ideally those in government or power should be conscious of their religious and social responsibility towards their people. Such a government works to preserve the fabric of society and champion justice for all, without marginalizing any minori-ties or alienating the opposition. Nonetheless, when social justice is employed by a community, regardless of the form of government that rules over them, it strengthens that community.

When it comes to those in government and positions of au-thority, they must understand that they cannot treat people as mere numbers. A ruler must understand that he is not a machine nor are his citizens objects that can be disposed of. Both the legislation and execution of the laws must be based on moral values and principles that aim to protect the rights and liberties of the people. If a person in office devi-ates from the principles established to protect the people, he is responsible for other deviations that trickle down the chain of leadership in the system of governance. Instead of a government that collectively protects and serves its people, society would be left with corruption and tyranny because of the actions of a few at the very top. Those in positions of leadership can curtail this if they follow the specific directives of Imam Ali.

> Do not say, 'I have been given command so that my commands may be obeyed,' as that will corrupt your heart, weaken your faith, and a draw you closer to [unwanted] change.[5]

These instructions are a reminder of the serious ramifications of authoritative abuse where the objective of governorship is altered from service to subjugation. The consequences of tyranny have a devastating impact on the oppressed and the oppressor. People suffer psychologically, financially, and morally when their rights are violated and their liberties are stripped away from them. With no lament from the oppressor, it is important to realize what detriment he will experience due to his choices.

One, a leader that employs perverted means to reach his goals may achieve his desires but will lose the purity of his heart. His heart will grow darker each day as he immerses himself further and further into sin. Though he may see material gains from his moral deviation, it will bring him unease and distress. True tranquility and comfort is not seen except by those with a whole moral conscience. Two, cor-

---

[5] Ibid.

ruption wreaks more corruption. Within that sphere of deviance, leaders tend to justify their actions no matter how bad it may get. This will in turn affect their own lens of discerning what is true and false, and what is right and wrong. Three, such individuals will find instability as a constant theme particular in their emotions and relationships. When truth and justice do not play a role in a person's life, psychology instability takes charge. With a lack of commitment to people and honoring relationships with them, the leader only exposes himself further to retribution from the people that he rules over. People do not forget a person who violates their rights and transgresses against their life, liberty, or property.

Imam Ali advised his representative in Azerbaijan, Al-Ash'ath Ibn Qais, like he advised his other ambassadors and governors. He instructed Ibn Qais on the nature of his assignment.

> *Certainly, your assignment is not a morsel for you, but it is a trust around your neck, and you have been charged with the protection [of the people] on behalf of your superiors. It is not for you to be oppressive towards the ruled, nor to take risks unless on strong grounds.[6]*

The Commander of the Faithful reminded Ibn Qais that positions of authority are not perpetual and administrative changes are inevitable. Thus, a person in charge must be ready at all times to be questioned as he is accountable be-

---

[6] Ibid, 3:6, Letter 5.

fore those he governs. In this life, he must be prepared to be transparent and open his books if he is investigated. And even if he is not questioned in this world, he cannot escape accountability before God on the Day of Judgement, as is mentioned in the following verses. "On that day you shall be exposed to view-no secret of yours shall remain hidden,"[7]

> *And certainly you have come to Us alone as We created you at first, and you have left behind your backs the things which We gave you, and We do not see with you your intercessors about whom you asserted that they were [God's] associates in respect to you; certainly the ties between you are now cut off and what you asserted is gone from you.*[8]

We are all responsible and accountable for our actions. Persons in positions of authority are especially accountable to those their leadership touches. They are not immune from questioning or liability. Thus, they need to be aware of every decision they make and action they pursue. Accountability to the public is truly one of the most sensitive positions to be in. It cannot be toyed with or taken lightly. Transparency is a must and integrity will be one's only savior. If accountability is observed with leaders at the highest level, its effect will also trickle down to the chain of leadership and representation in the governing body. If corruption can be emulated, so can virtue. Appointees and employees will be deterred from engaging in corruption or fraud because they

---

[7] The Holy Quran, 69:18.
[8] The Holy Quran, 6:94.

witnessed the implications of such actions with their superiors. They will develop a greater sense of responsibility for their people and nations. All this will contribute to a substantial reduction in corruption in the system of governance.

Equally important to those in authority are the people who are responsible for ensuring accountability. Individuals in working in auditing and investigative bodies that monitor the functions of other groups or bodies of authority hold a great deal of weight. From their positions they must be vigilant in detecting corruption, while providing guidance and constructive advice to those in leadership. They are some of the most important instrument of change and reform in any system. Such positions may exist internally, within an organization, institution, or government, or even externally. Their utilization of performance evaluations is particularly key for the assessment of growth, productivity, and waste. Such evaluations can also be the basis for financial incentives and promotions within an organization or institution.

Imam Ali advocated for these practices because he viewed them as essential for the growth and progress of the community. He stressed the importance of constructive criticism and objective evaluations rooted in qualifications, integrity, and citizenship. The Imam said,

> *If the ruled fulfill the rights of the ruler and the ruler fulfills their rights, then right attains the position of honor among them, the ways of religion become established, signs of justice become fixed and the precedence will continue. In this way*

time will improve, the continuance of government will be ex-
pected, and the aims of the enemies will be frustrated.[9]

We understand from these words that responsibility is
shared between the governor and the governed. The underlying objective should be advancing the common good. It
then flows naturally that though there may be different
groups and factions within a community, they must nonetheless collaborate and work together on common interests
for the collective. Every person should assume his responsibility and fulfil his role toward the greater good. All members of the community should uphold common values, act
with sincerity and honesty, and preserve the rights of the
public. They should remain steadfast in working together
within this framework and not compromise these values.
Such an outlook and means of engagement is both a religious and civic duty.

To further these goals, it is important to realize that we
need to be courageous enough to provide and receive mean-
ingful advice and guidance. Open and respectful dialogue is
instrumental in addressing the problems we face as a community and resolving the disputes that arise amongst us.
Adamancy and rigidity will only perpetuate the challenges
we face, while flexibility and openness helps people move
past their differences and come closer to commonalities and
collaboration. When we remain open to seeking what is bet-

---

[9] Al-Radhi, *Nahj Al-Balagha*, 2:199, Sermon 216.

ter and understanding the truth, we can hear each other that much clearer.

> *The person who feels disgusted when truth is said to him or a just matter is placed before him would find it more difficult to act upon them. Therefore, do not abstain from saying a truth or pointing out a matter of justice...*[10]

Imam Ali warned us about the dangers of disregarding the truth. He emphasized the importance for us to train our minds and souls to accept the truth and not rebel against guidance. The Imam focused on the psyche as it plays a consequential role in impacting conduct and behavior. If a person is prepared psychologically for a certain action, he is more likely to actually follow through in executing the act. Psychological readiness is usually a prerequisite for physical action. This applies with things ranging from consuming medication and eating healthy to refraining from sin and breaking bad habits. Similarly, if a person in power is mentally convinced about the value of change and reform, he will be more willing to relinquish his power, even if part of him resents doing so.

LEADERSHIP THROUGH JUSTICE

Leadership is a great responsibility, and we all lead in the system of our lives in different capacities. When it comes to assigning others in positions of leadership, it should be based on certain prerequisites that demonstrate qualification

---

[10] Ibid.

for that position. In emphasizing qualification, as opposed to nepotism or relationship, justice can be more readily seen in society. The more sensitive or consequential a position is, the more demanding the qualifications should be. This becomes increasingly important when the job is serving and helping people. There should be no room for negligence in selecting unqualified candidates or allowing for subpar appointees to continue in their positions. The Commander of the Faithful Imam Ali discusses this.

> The worst minister for you is he who has been a minister for mischievous persons before you, and who joined them in sins. Therefore, he should not be your chief man, because they are abettors of sinners and brothers of the oppressors. You can find good substitutes for them who will be like them in their views and influence, while not being like them in sins and vices. They have never assisted an oppressor in his oppression or a sinner in his sin.[11]

Imam Ali makes three points in this part of his instructions to Malik Al-Ashtar. First, it is imperative to ensure that a minister does not have a history of oppression or aiding the actions of oppressors. Second, it is vital for a governor to continuously discover new talents and resources. A position should never be monopolized by a particular person or group. The standard for qualifications should be that the candidate meets the credentials for the job, is upright and honest, and does not have a history of vice. He should be

---

[11] Ibid, 2:199, Letter 53.

assessed and rewarded for his credentials and commitment. Third, leaders should not resort to or provide a platform for individuals implicated in oppression. Such individuals can play a damaging role in the consultations they provide and effect they have on decision-makers around them. The people sought should be upright and respected for their virtue and integrity. Imam Ali states, "The most pleasant thing for [leaders] is the establishment of justice in their areas and the manifestation of love from their [citizens]."[12] The best means to achieve stability and security, without fear of a revolt or coup, is by instilling justice and fairness through protecting people's rights and liberties. At that point, there is no reason for people to oppose or take a stand against the governing body. Instead, they will love their leadership and willingly follow it. The equation is simple: the government cares for its constituents and in return the people will be loyal and faithful.

Nonetheless, justice is inherently good to establish. A leader should uphold justice even if he does not fear revolt. Justice should be upheld as opposed to being complacent with injustice, because incidents of injustice are manifestations of oppression abhorred by God.

> *Do justice to God and do justice towards the people, as against yourself, your near ones and those of your subjects for whom you have a liking. Surely, if you do not do so you will be oppressive, and when a person oppresses the creatures*

---

[12] Ibid.

*of God then God becomes his opponent and not God's crea-
tures. When God is the opponent of a person He tramples
his plea; and he will remain in the position of being at war
with God until he gives it up and repents. Nothing is more
inducive of the reversal of God's bounty or for the hastening
of His retribution than continuance in oppression. Surely,
God hears the prayer of the oppressed and is on the look-out
for the oppressors.*[13]

The Imam focused on the word 'al-insaf' which translates to
'fairness'. It is defined in *Taj Al-'Aroos*, an Arabic diction-
ary, as taking the truth and granting the truth. Imam Ali
warned against disturbing the balance where the sources of
decision-making are influenced by inappropriate factors
such that they lose their credibility and become oppressive
and unjust. "Beware of disobeying God in solitude, because
the witness [of the sin] is also the judge,"[14] Imam Ali
warned. Governors, rulers, leaders, and all people that hold
authority over others should be forewarned that they cannot
escape God's judgment. No wealth, power, or army can
help him when he faces God's wrath. The only means to
salvation is repentance, and such repentance can only come
through humility, admitting one's faults, and swearing never
to return.

Consequently, reason should drive persons of position to be
cautious about making mistakes leading to injustice as "God

---

13 Ibid.
14 Ibid, 532, Tradition 324.

does not love the unjust,"[15]and because "surely the iniqui-
tous shall remain in lasting chastisement."[16] God reminds us
about punishment so we can awake from our heedlessness
before it is too late and we drown in our sin. The Imam
speaks about the danger following one's desires in his letter
to Al-Aswad Ibn Qutbah, the governor of Hulwan.

> *If a governor engages in his desires, they will impede him
> from implementing the greater part of justice. All people
> should be equal in right before you, for surely injustice can-
> not be a substitute for justice.*[17]

Persons in power are entrusted with exercising justice. They
have an obligation to make justice reign by ensuring that
people's rights and freedoms are protected. Naturally, there
needs to be some form of monitoring and supervision to
guarantee this responsibility is fulfilled. During his tenure as
caliph, Imam Ali paid close attention to the conduct of his
appointees and representatives. It was not enough to merely
hold a position under a just government, those who held
positions needed to reflect the justice that government
claimed to espouse. At one point, Imam Ali reprimanded
his appointed governor in Basra, Othman Ibn Hunayf Al-
Ansari, for conduct that he saw unbecoming of a leader in
his administration.

> *O Ibn Hunayf, I have come to know that a young man of
> Basrah invited you to a feast and you leapt towards it.*

---

15 The Holy Quran, 3:57.
16 The Holy Quran, 42:45.
17 Al-Radhi, *Nahj Al-Balagha*, 115-116, Letter 59.

Foods of different colors were being chosen for you and big bowls were being given to you. I never thought that you would accept the feast of a people who turn down the beggars and invite the rich.[18]

Imam Ali's letter to Ibn Hunayf provides great insight for a student of leadership and just governance. First, he is making it clear that a position of power is a responsibility and not a privilege. Second, a ruler is responsible for the affairs of his constituents, irrespective of where they are at. That is why we find that Imam Ali's criticism of Ibn Hunayf did not specify the people of Basra or any other geographical location. The Imam reprimanded Ibn Hunayf for attending a function that was selective and exclusive. His concern was that Ibn Hunayf was tending to the whims of elitists rather than giving his time and attention to the general public – those who he is tasked to serve.

Third, the Imam was troubled by the precedent that Ibn Hunayf was setting by attending a function that intentionally excluded the underserved. As a governor and leader, Ibn Hunayf is inadvertently endorsing the discriminatory actions of the organizers of the event. This is a form of oppression and injustice against the underprivileged. Furthermore, these bigoted practices can fracture the fabric of the community and fuel tension that further distress the social relations between the different factions in the community. Ibn Hunayf should have been cognizant of all of these consider-

---

[18] Ibid, 115-116, Letter 45.

ations and thus, made a more responsible decision in rejecting the invite.

The pain of oppression and injustice are severe. Imam Ali did not want anyone under his leadership to endure that pain. He did everything in his capacity to instill and implement justice. The Commander of the Faithful monitored his governors and provided them with ongoing advice and instructions. He did not shy away from reprimanding them, as he did with Othman Ibn Hunayf. The Imam's goal was setting the standard of just governance. He provided the model government for people to assess those that came before and those that would come after. It was a government concerned with administering justice and equity. It worked for and with its constituency to protect their rights and advance their interests. It honored the shared responsibility for establishing justice and reminded people of it as advised in the Holy Quran, "And stop them, for they shall be questioned."[19] The government and leadership of Imam Ali was that virtuous system run by a moral compass invested in protecting others before oneself. It was one that continued the Prophet's vision of bringing prosperity through virtue and moderation.

---

[19] The Holy Quran, 37:24.

MODERATION FOR PROSPERITY

BALANCE FOR PROSPERITY

Moderation is the key to success and prosperity. It is an essential component in practicing justice and bringing about solid leadership. Our faith chooses moderation and abhors any form of extremism. When extremism is rejected and moderation is adopted, people enjoy their equality in humanity and are saved from racial, ethnic, and social discrimination. Though people may naturally distinguish themselves from others by their accomplishments or affiliations, it does not mean they can demean others or violate their rights in any way. Superiority is in nothing but piety and if one is pious then he does not claim superiority. In order for a person to become pious, he must honor the rights of his fellow and work to protect and serve others before even before himself. The Commander of the Faithful said as he was building the foundation for moderation, "So, extend to them your forgiveness and pardon, in the same way as you would like God to extend His forgiveness and pardon to you…"[1]

To exercise moderation, a leader must be fair and ensure the protection of people's due rights. If we desire for God to forgive us for our shortcomings, we must be willing to forgive others for theirs. This becomes increasingly important for someone who assumes a position of power or authority and is thus expected to lead by example. A leader should be at the forefront in establishing a culture of forgiveness and forbearance. As mentioned previously in the discussion on justice, the actions of a leader trickle down to the chain of leadership – whether the action is good or bad, it trickles down.

Creating a culture that transcends grudges and practices forbearance instead will transform the way people deal with conflict in society. Tensions will diffuse and enmity will lessen. Cooperation and collaboration for moving the community forward can be actualized to a larger extent. People are diverse in their backgrounds, experience, and ideas. There is bound to be some forms of disagreement or conflict, and we all make mistakes. If we are not willing to become tolerant of one another and move beyond our mistakes and differences, we will not be able to thrive as a community.

---

[1] Al-Radhi, *Nahj Al-Balagha*, 3:84, Letter 53.

As part of his will to his son Imam Hassan, Imam Ali instructs,

> *Make yourself the measure for dealings between you and others. Thus, you should wish for others what you wish for yourself and hate for others what you hate for yourself. Do not oppress as you do not like to be oppressed. Do good deeds for others as you like goodness to be done to you. Regard as bad for yourself whatever you regard as bad for others. Accept from others what you like others to accept from you.[2]*

The Imam lays out a plan based on a core principle – moderation. The Imam advised that people be balanced in their relationships. A balanced relationship is one that is compatible with our nature and reason such that good is desired and evil is abhorred. With balance, mutual respect is adopted and favoritism is neglected. Having balance in relationships often renders closer and more long-lasting connections to people. With moderation and balance you enter people's hearts because you have gained their trust and confidence. Imam Ali kept this in perspective telling us to, "Live amongst people in such a manner that if you die they weep over you and if you are alive they long for you."[3]

One of the overarching principles that the Imam drove was inclusion. Imam Ali was an advocate for a society that embraces diversity. It is only natural for a community to be di-

---

[2] Ibid, 3:45-46.
[3] Ibid, 4:4, Hadith 10.

verse in race, religion, ethnicity, and socio-economic status. People will always be different and thus, in order to have a harmonious and productive community, people have to focus on the commonalties that bring them together and promote the common good. That does not mean that people ought to forgo their distinctions in belief and identity, and assimilate into their society's melting pot. We do not believe that compromising one's identity or beliefs is necessary to successfully engage with others and build a community.

We can achieve both through integration. The key here is to actively engage in society, respecting and tolerating others that are different from us, while demanding that same respect and tolerance for our own differences in beliefs and identity. This culture of inclusion requires people to respect each other's differences and deal with one another with compassion. Otherwise, people will inadvertently resort to means of exclusion where the strong oppress the weak and the majority disregards the minority. With that approach, tyranny rules and people are persecuted for their creed, nationality, ethnicity, or mere expression. The Commander of the Faithful warned against this repulsive culture. In sermon 141, Imam Ali told his people,

> *O people! If a person knows his brother to be steadfast in faith and of correct ways, he should not lend ear to what people may say about him. Sometimes the bowman shoots arrows but the arrow goes astray; similarly talk can be off*

the point.... There is nothing between truth and falsehood except four fingers.

The Imam was asked the meaning of this whereupon he joined his fingers together and put them between his ear and eye and said: It is falsehood when you say, 'I have heard so,' while it is truth when you say, 'I have seen.'[4]

The Imam's priority was to protect people and safeguard their rights. This requires that one deliberates, investigates, and reaches certainty before making a judgment against any person. There is no need for hasty and rash judgements that can lead to irreparable harm such as taking the life of an innocent human being. Be it in positions of official judgment and execution, or in our daily affairs as ordinary citizens, we must exercise patience and engage in constructive dialogue as the Holy Quran teaches.

Call to the way of your Lord with wisdom and goodly exhortation, and have disputations with them in the best manner; surely your Lord best knows those who go astray from His path, and He knows best those who follow the right way.[5]

If you want to be an effective communicator, you must exhibit politeness and courtesy. There is no benefit in stultifying and demeaning others.

Even when it comes to enjoining in good and forbidding evil, there are specific guidelines that must be followed so

---

[4] Ibid, 2:24, Sermon 141.
[5] The Holy Quran, 16:125.

time and effort is not wasted. The key is there needs to be constructive dialogue in which the other person is acknowledged and respected. Otherwise, if the other person feels degraded or marginalized, he will not be receptive and listen to what you have to say of guidance or goodness. Our Islamic teachings emphasize good manners. A person must work diligently to instill in himself good manners. It is an ongoing process in which a person ought to train himself to be conscious of his behavior and attitude. Our conduct is a reflection of our attitude and mindset. We have to start by respecting ourselves and taking responsibility for our own actions, and that does not come without owning a positive attitude. If we respect ourselves, we will respect others and treat them with honor and dignity. Mutual respect is the main ingredient for peace and coexistence to thrive in a society. Imam Ali has countless sayings that touch on different aspects of ethics and manners.

> *Cheerfulness is the bond of friendship.[6] Loving one another is half of wisdom.[7] Justice results in more close friends.[8] If you cannot forbear, feign to do so.[9] Habituate your heart to mercy for the subjects...[10] The highest act of a noble person is to ignore what he knows.[11]*

---

6 Al-Radhi, *Nahj Al-Balagha*, 4:4, Hadith 10.

7 Ibid, 4:34, Hadith 142.

8 Ibid, 4:50, Hadith 224.

9 Ibid, 4:47, Hadith 206.

10 Ibid, 3:84, Letter 53.

11 Ibid, 4:50, Hadith 222.

ETHICS AND VIRTUE

The Commander of the Faithful desired for people to embrace and adopt noble attributes. He worked to establish a culture of virtue where people, young and old, upheld themselves to a higher standard of ethics and virtue. The Imam focused on a number of specific attributes and actions that he wanted his followers to espouse. First, for people to engage with each another with positivity, cheerfulness, and smiles. Second, to use language that conveys respect and friendliness. Third, to uphold and implement justice. Imam Ali urged people to be positive mediators between parties of conflict and to use their influence to resolve disputes and mend broken relationships. In order to exercise this critical role, one has to maintain his impartiality and independence of any external social pressures. He needs to exhibit high morals by being merciful, benevolent, and forbearing. By making it a priority to uphold these virtues and working to get rid of one's vices, a person has set a steady course on the path of leadership and development.

The Commander of the Faithful warns against characteristics which conflict with moderation and prevent one from reaching his excellence. He states,

> *He who goes too far in quarrelling is a sinner, but if one falls short in it, one is oppressed and it is difficult for a quarreler to fear God...*[12] *Your turning away from he who inclines towards you is a loss of your fortune while your in-*

---

[12] Ibid, 4:72, Hadith 298.

clining towards he who turns away from you is humiliation for yourself...[13] It is enough for your own discipline that you abstain from what you dislike from others.[14]

If a person refrains from falling into any of the negative behaviors described by the narrations above, he is closer to having moderation in his life. Love will replace hatred and connecting to people will be that much easier. Next, he will refrain from being insistent and taking inflexible positions out of mere stubbornness which leads to transgression and oppression. Additionally, one will be balanced in his positions where he will avoid degrading others by using them or be degraded by others using him. Finally, a person can avoid falling into what he criticizes others for and repeating their mistakes. This cannot be achieved by isolating oneself from the community around him, with the effort to avoid their mistakes or dissolving into their practices and way of life. Instead, we should engage and integrate to protect ourselves and advance our cause. Imam Ali said, "Nearness with people in their manners brings about safety from their troubles."[15]

It is imperative for people to open channels of communication and build bridges. This will render positive relationships that can lead to mutual cooperation. However, in our engagement we need to be careful not to immerse ourselves blindly with others. Like anything else, balance is the key.

---

13 Ibid, 4:104, Hadith 451.
14 Ibid, 4:96, Hadith 412.
15 Ibid, 4:94, Hadith 401.

Associating with others can render great benefits. We can learn from each other's' experiences and benefit from our relationships alleviate certain problems and threats. On the other hand, there are drawbacks to engaging with others if a person mismanages the relationship. In one of the Imam's letters to his son Al-Hassan he advises him,

> *Bear yourself towards your brother in such a way that when he disregards kinship, keep to it; when he turns away, be kind and draw near; when he withholds, give; when he grows far, approach; when he is harsh, be lenient; when he offends, forgive – so much so as though you are his servant and he is the benevolent master over you. But take care that this should not be done inappropriately, and that you should not behave so with an undeserving person.[16]*

God created us as social beings. We are designed to live, work, and associate with others, as integral parts of a greater community. In order for us to succeed in our lives we must be able to manage our relationships with others, instead of avoiding them altogether. Imam Ali teaches us to prioritize our ethics over anything else and seek our personal excellence. This requires that at times, we take the high road and be the better person in conflict or disagreement. However, we should be mindful as the Imam advises "not [to] behave so with an undeserving person." We need to use moderation to ensure that we do not come near oppression, nor should we allow for ourselves to be thrown into peril.

---

[16] Ibid, 3:53.

INTEGRITY FOR VIRTUE

Reform is not an easy task. It requires preparation and an atmosphere that is ready to accept change. Before a reformer can institute reform anywhere, he must set the platform and prepare the right environment for his message to be received. Negativity cannot reign in such an environment, nor can vice and corruption. People that want change want it to better what already exists. It needs an environment that will be responsive to such a desire, because a reformer cannot bring change without some foundation of goodness.

To have that environment, a reformer must first impart the principles of virtue in himself before he can work on others. Next, he ought to establish the principles of integrity and trust in the public sphere such that it becomes the commodity that people use to engage and transact with one another. Integrity and trust are essential for the continuity of healthy engagement between people. It is essential in developing one's character and morality, which is the cornerstone for building a society of 'God's dependents.' The Prophet is narrated to have said, "Creations are God's dependents...

the most loved by God are those who are most useful to His dependents."[1]

The key is to establish a culture of integrity. To create a culture, you need action to commit to principle and constant redirection for guidance. If you do not have that, immorality and misfortune will naturally take the place of the virtue and integrity we desire. Thus, it becomes imperative to champion reform through enjoining in good and forbidding evil. Enjoining in good and forbidding evil is an ongoing process that transcends time and place. It is subjective to the circumstances at the time. Every person can partake through their own capacity. It is the means to establish social justice, alleviate oppression, and ensure that society is on the right course. The Holy Prophet said, "O people, be careful of oppression, for oppression will be darkness on the Day of Judgement."[2]

Imam Hussain addressed some of these problems and offered effective solutions for them. He did this particularly, and with some detail, in a sermon he delivered on morals and virtues. As an immaculate exemplar of prophetic morals and values, people revere the Imam and look up to him as a leader and guide. People during his time and much after take his word and acknowledge its great weight. They realize his role and appreciate that his concern was for the people's wellbeing and only desires that which is best for them. Many nations struggle from individuals that attempt to

---

[1] Al-Radhi, *Al-Mujazat Al-Nabawiya*, 241-242.

[2] Ahmad ibn Hanbal, *Musnad Ahmad*, 2:107.

champion reform in society when they are lacking the vision, knowhow, or skill to succeed. Thus, their propositions are incomplete or flawed. However, the Imam encompassed all the virtuous attributes needed to be that example of reform and excellence. For that, he was a vicegerent of God and a guardian of the Prophet's message.

> O you who believe, obey God and obey the Messenger and those in authority from among you; then if you quarrel about anything, refer it to God and the Messenger, if you believe in God and the last day; this is better and very good in the end.[3]

Like their father Imam Ali, Imam Hussain and his blessed progeny are the custodians of the Holy Prophet's message. The Prophet told his followers, "My family is like Ark of Noah. Whoever sets upon it will be saved and whoever abandons it will drown."[4] In embracing the words and directives of the Imam, we prepare ourselves to set sail with their blessed ship.

THE SERMON ON MORALS AND VIRTUES

In Imam Hussain's famous "Sermon on Morals and Values," he spoke at length on what and how people should engage as ethical members of their society. Below is a segment of the sermon that we should reflect on individually and as a community.

---

[3] The Holy Quran, 4:59.
[4] Al-Hakim Al-Nisabouri, *Al-Mustadrak*, 2:334.

O people, compete in doing good. Strive in [attaining] the reward [for doing good deeds]. Do not be satisfied in doing good when you did not initiate it. Attain praise for your success in [doing good] and do not get criticism for procrastinating [and failing in doing good]. If someone was to do a favor for a person and he knows that the person will not be able to repay it, God will repay him, for [God] is the most Generous and most Rewarding.

And know that doing good will render praise and reward. For if you were to see favor [i.e. doing good] as a man, you would find him pleasant and beautiful, delighting the observers. And if you were to observe malice [as a man], you would see him unpleasant and ugly such that the hearts repel him and the eyes turn away [in disgust] ...

Whomever strives for God the Most Exalted by doing good towards his brother, God will reward him during his time of need and alleviate some trials of this world which will exceed [the favors] he did.

And whomever alleviates the adversity of a believer, God the Exalted will relieve him from the troubles of this life and the hereafter. Whomever does good, God will do good towards him and God loves the good-doers.[5]

Al-Arbaly, a prominent Shia Muslim scholar, provides some insight on the advice of Imam Hussain through a comment in his book Kashf Al-Ghuma. He says,

---

[5] Al-Arbaly, *Kashf Al-Ghuma*, 2:239-240.

I have shared this segment of the Imam's words [i.e. Sermon on Morals and Virtues] ... although it is indicative of [the Imam's] eloquence and skillful expressive language, it is also indicative of his generosity, forbearance, and his beneficence. It is telling about the nobleness of his morals and conduct, and pure intentions. It is a testament of his benevolence and compassion. This segment [of the Imam's sermon] encompasses virtues and morals [to the extent] where all characteristics related to doing good are included. It contains extraordinary virtues. However, it is no surprise that these [extraordinary] merits are all there [pointing to the Imam].[6]

This segment from Imam Hussain's Sermon on Morals and Virtues includes a number of issues that are particularly important for us to reflect and implement individually. They are equally essential on a collective community level. These principles empower a community to instill change that will help it discover its potential and reflect strength and ability. The community will be able to do good, advance, innovate, and prosper. The Imam's nine principles provide a framework that guides people on how they should deal with one another and how to organize their internal and external affairs. It is a guide for establishing a culture of integrity so virtue can reign in our society. It also lays the foundation for how our communities can establish strong relationships with other communities by embracing universal human values. This has positive implications between communities of the same nation, as well as nation-to-nation relationships.

---

[6] Ibid.

With the universal values advocated we are mandated to re-spect treaties and agreements between various nations. The result of which will be mutual respect found on shared val-ues and the hopes for collaboration on growth and devel-opment. Stability and peace will be established through new means that will call for:

1. Bringing our communities honor and dignity
2. Working and being compensated justly
3. Relying on real accomplishments and not mere aspi-rations and dreams
4. Receiving praise for increasing production and effi-ciency as opposed to laziness and procrastination
5. Managing positions of responsibility and under-standing accountability
6. Reinforcing the value of doing good for it is a means of promotion in this life and credit for good deeds in the hereafter
7. Activating our moral dimension as a means of im-pact for solving complex problems
8. Resolving a problem for a fellow believer will help resolve our own personal problems in this life and hereafter
9. Reciprocating good with good, and God loves the good-doers

In adopting this mechanism for dealing with others, there are positive gains that will render benefits for everyone. First, an individual will embrace personal accountability and thus, will not need to be supervised by a superior or followed by surveillance. One will realize that any position he assumes – at a school, university, mosque, factory, farm, hospital, government agency, etc. – is in reality a responsibility and not merely a space to fill. Whatever position we assume is a privilege and blessing from God. We need to be grateful for that, otherwise the blessing will leave us for someone who will appreciate it. The Commander of the Faithful says, "Beware of repelling blessings for not every escapee can be returned."[7]

Imam Ali showed that goodness and malice are both characteristics in the human being. One must strive to activate goodness and quell desires opposed to it. We have the ability to decide for ourselves what course we wish to take. We charter our path through the choices we make. God gave us that free will and we are responsible for it. On that day when money, wealth, and children will render us no protection or benefit – all that will be there for us are our deeds. The Holy Quran describes this epic day.

> *And the day when the unjust one shall bite his hands saying, O would that I had taken a way with the Messenger. O woe is me, would that I had not taken such a one for a friend. Certainly he led me astray from the reminder after it had come to me, and Satan fails to aid man.*[8]

In his sermon, Imam Hussain analogizes goodness and malice to two men of contradicting appearances and effects on

---

[7] Al-Radhi, *Nahj Al-Balagha*, 4:54.
[8] The Holy Quran, 25:27-29.

people. He artistically conveys the value of doing good and urges people to choose the beauty of goodness over the dread of malice. Every person can be like the beautiful man who delights the observers and exceeds the scholars with his generosity. At the same time, a person can decide to be like the ugly man that repels others' hearts and eyes with his malice. The decision is ours.

We find that the Imam used this analogy to warn us from falling into committing wrong. When people have a desire to do good, they will be able to utilize their talents and capabilities in all facets of life. When people are spirited to act, productivity will increase because the thought is coupled with passion. From one individual to another, there will be a positive domino effect. This will also result in the economic growth required for the security and stability of a community, let alone a nation. With economic growth that touches all levels of society there comes social stability. This is particularly important because when everyone in society is lifted, class structure and the ails that accompany it will dwindle. If social class structure is chipped away, more people will be engaged in the process because they will find hope and opportunity. This will produce an environment in which there is more optimism and desire to do good which will help propel the community forward.

With this, the Imam painted a clear picture of what a good Muslim looks like. One who rids himself from any vice that can contaminate his character, such as malice. Malice is an abhorred quality used to describe someone who is 'stingy and undignified."[9] A true Muslim is one who expresses kindness and engages in doing good.

Through his words, the Imam plants the spirit of virtue and goodness in people. He wanted to inspire people to embrace a lifestyle of service. Whether it is helping an underprivileged person through financial support or fulfilling a request for someone in desperate need, the key is to offer genuine service. The Imam teaches us to not take advantage of others by exploiting them during their time of need or using service to advance personal agendas. That is not the service that the Imam is advocating for.

The underlying objective that Imam had in delivering this powerful sermon was to build a culture of integrity. A culture in which individuals realize and embrace the value of kindness, compassion, and service. A culture that transcends time and place and carries on from one generation to the other. In order for this culture to continue to grow and prosper, the key is that people give with no strings attached. They do good and do not expect repayment or gratitude because the ultimate reward is from God. The Holy Prophet said, "Do good for those who are deserving and undeserving, for even if you do good towards someone that is undeserving, you are surely deserving to do good."[10] When the culture of goodness and service perpetuates in society, people will be less likely to fall to corruption, bribery, and extortion. There will be a greater sense of responsibility and

---

[9] Ibn Fares, *Maqaees Al-Lugha*, 5:226.
[10] Al-Sadooq, *Iyoun Akhbar Al-Rida*, 1:38.

accountability, especially in the public sector. This will render more trust and contentment amongst people, which is essential for a thriving community.

INTEGRITY AND JURISPRUDENCE

Islamic jurisprudence addresses the matter of integrity and some of the violations that are associated with it such as financial corruption. Beyond discussing the ethical implications of integrity, or the lack thereof, it is essential to research the laws associated with integrity. Though it is not the focus of our discussion here, it is important to end the chapter with some brief thoughts on the laws relating to integrity as a means to encourage the reader to do further research to be informed on these issues.

Financial corruption, and corruption generally, originates from various sources and manifests itself in countless ways. However, the reason behind it is one – lack of willpower and deterioration of integrity. People compromise their integrity for numerous reasons. Some are willing to take bribes because they face financial struggles. Others are greedy and leverage their power to make extra cash. Another reason behind financial corruption can be politically motivated where ruling elites abuse their power to score personal gains. Even worse is when the judiciary who is assigned to carry the mantle of justice is corrupt and itself engages in bribery and extortion. Finally, sometimes corruption finds its way due to poor leadership and mismanagement.

Nonetheless, all of these violations can lead to criminal prosecution. Different forms of financial corruption such as embezzlement and fraud are all manifestations of financial and administrative deviance. It is usually carried by an individual or a group of individuals who conspire to leverage their power and exploit opportunities. These are serious crimes, both religiously and civilly, and are intolerable in our faith.

Islamic jurisprudence addresses all of these matters by taking a firm position forbidding general and specific acts that undermine integrity and perpetuate corruption. Just to illustrate some examples, on a general level, cheating and bribery are strictly forbidden acts. More specifically, Islamic law specifically forbids misappropriating public money for personal use and breaching employment contracts, as well as breaching any legitimate contract between parties. All of these laws are intended to protect and advance the state of the people by promoting a culture of morality and good dealings while protecting people's rights.

INTELLECT ENGAGED

INSPIRATION FROM IMAM AL-SADIQ

Human beings are civil by nature. They gravitate towards others and seek to communicate and express. As human beings, we have this dire need to be completed by one another as individuals. At the same time, we seek to benefit from one another's experiences to add to our own experience and knowledge-base.

There are varying levels of communication and connection that take place between us. For one there is the connection that takes place between generations through thought, tradition, and culture. These elements link the current generation to its rich past, part of which represents an important segment of their deep history. As generations look back into their history, connecting with the generations that have past, they can see a great deal of experience and wisdom to be gained. Their knowledge, of course, does not replace the importance of experience to be had in the present; however, it brings lessons and guidance that can help provide for better decision-making in the future. Thus, it is vital that this connection between the past and present remains. This relationship can bring forth much in benefit.

There are new challenges upon us in every modern era, that must be faced with certainty and using all the past experience we have to best address them. We cannot neglect the past, nor can we completely rely on it. Past knowledge cannot replace what we are ignorant of today. This would certainly cause worry and concern for the state of the future. Holding on to heritage, of what it holds of experience and wisdom, is necessary. There are particular strengths that come from one's rich heritage. Much of what we have of ethics and manners comes from our heritage and tradition. It also allows for natural growth through the experiences of the past by which individuals and communities grow stronger.

Of the most prominent positions of strength that exist within Islamic heritage is what has been narrated of guidance and directives from Imam Ja'far Al-Sadiq. His leadership and inspiration has illuminated the path for people striving to advance themselves, and their communities, for centuries. His commitment to improving the human condition, as well as providing a unique balance for the development of mind, body, and spirit, is an inspiration to Muslims and non-Muslims alike. For his method and discourse is universal, one that applies to anyone concerned with human development and progress for all. His style of leadership, as well as the principles he emphasized, enfranchised people regardless of their racial, ethnic, or religious backgrounds. The encompassing nature of his school of thought did not dilute the principles or identity of the school; rather, it strengthened it and made it stand out for its uniqueness. The Ja'fari school did not compromise its identity or creed. It did, however, ensure that its objective was to empower and advance all – for the overarching goal was the development of humanity. With all the challenges faced at that time, of socio-political pressure and persecution, the enlightenment of Imam Al-Sadiq continued to shine people's paths.

The school of thought sought to advance people in all fields of science and learning. Of the thousands of students that encircled Imam Al-Sadiq in the Grand Mosque of Kufa, many would come out to be pioneers in chemistry, physics, history, astronomy, ethics and jurisprudence. Imam Al-Sadiq was that all-encompassing leader, scholar, and teacher. He provided what people needed for their spiritual, intellectual, and material development. It was not merely through the principles and theory he taught, but through the practical example he established and his presence as the exemplar of ethics and virtue for his society. Human development was part and parcel to the programs of the Imam. As an overarching goal of education and engagement, he secured the balance necessary for people to realize that success can be achieved in this world and the next.

This school of thought has endured much in trials and tribulations over the years. It triumphed over existential threats, ones that wished to disable or terminate its role in society. By the grace of God, it was able to persevere through all of that and carry on. Imam Al-Sadiq was able to protect the principles of the Prophet, both in and out of the mosque, and help in societal reform. He guided their thought, penetrated their habits, and empowered them to hold on to whatever ethics and good practices they had.

As an exemplar of virtue and ethics, the Imam genuinely cared for people and showed it in practice. He walked humbly and did not seek fame. He aided the poor and the weak. He gave a lending hand wherever was needed. At the same time, his prestige and presence was felt wherever he went. He was not hesitant or timid, nor did he fear those who differed with him or wished him ill. The spirit of his engagement was the spirit of humanity, inspired by the spirit of God. In that, he cared deeply for people's souls, growing their potential, and empowering their abilities towards betterment. At the same time, he focused on increasing their aptitude for tolerance and engagement with people from different backgrounds. Naturally such interaction is a part of life. He promoted diversity and engagement, without melting into a counterpart's identity. Integration while preserving one's identity was key.

His encompassing and inclusive style of engagement and leadership attracted many to follow his school his thought, even if they did not believe in some of its foundations or principles. Here, people found what they could not in other schools of thought. Depth in thought, intricate knowledge, and objective discourse were uniquely characteristic of the Ja'fari school. These traits are definitely universal human values, and for that people were attracted to this school of thought. Those values were embodied in the person of Imam Al-Sadiq.

People involved in the pursuit of knowledge and intellectual engagement could see the clear difference between him and the others that promoted themselves within the domain of religion and scholarship. His character and virtue, let alone his knowledge, set him apart. He needed to say nothing of those around him, his actions spoke much louder than any words. He did not need to create a ruckus or promote himself with people to gain a following. He worked honestly and quietly. For those paying attention, they saw what his school represented and how it stood out as the straight ruler that exposed the crookedness in the other lines.

PUTTING DEVELOPMENT INTO ACTION

Some of the self-declared scholars of the time would challenge Imam Al-Sadiq or put forth thoughts that contradicted the principles of Islam. Amongst them were Abdul Kareem ibn Abi Al-'Awjaa, whose ideas and propositions rode on the lines of heresy and skepticism. At one point he would talk to Imam Al-Sadiq mocking some of the most fundamental tenets of the faith. He said,

O Aba Abdillah[1] … for how long will you continue to thresh this threshing floor and tend to this rock? How long will you worship this house built of bricks and clay, and circulate around it like lost camels? There is someone who thought this out and made it up. He knew that this was an act created not by the wise nor one of vision. So speak, for you are the head and boss of this matter, and your father established it.[2]

His approach with the likes of Ibn Abi Al-'Awjaa was not to stoop down to their level of attacks and senseless talk. He spoke for those listening, then and now, more than he did for them particularly. His responses were scientific, measured, logical and founded in reason. To Ibn Abi Al-'Awjaa he said,

This house is one that God had His servants worship Him through to test their devotion in coming to Him. He ordered them to exalt it and visit it, making it the place for his prophets and the direction for those praying to Him. For it is a part of His pleasure and a way to attain His forgiveness. It was erected in the path of perfection and a gathering of greatness and majesty. God created it before the Earth by a thousand years. It is best that He is obeyed in what He has ordered and what He prohibited to refrain from for God enjoined the souls and their image.[3]

---

[1] Aba Abdillah was the kunya, or teknonym, of Imam Ja'far Al-Sadiq – usually the name of the eldest child.

[2] Al-Kulayni, *Al-Kafi*, 4:197, II. 1.

[3] Ibid.

The Imam's response was a lesson in the necessity of worship, carrying out the etiquette of thanking one who bestows us with goodness. God created His creation, founded them, and gave an image like no other; thus, the intellect dictates that we as creation would thank God for His generosity and mercy upon us in creating us. That is through our worship of Him and obeying His commandments. This is a simple, yet fundamental, belief that counters the stubbornness and negativity that some may propose in regards to acts of worship and rituals of prayer and supplication.

Abu Hanifa was quite bold, and imprudent, in his statements as well.

> *What does Ja'far ibn Muhammad know? I am more knowledgeable than he. I met the men [of narration] and heard from their mouths, while Ja'far ibn Muhammad is a mere reader who gained his knowledge from books.*[4]

When Imam Al-Sadiq was told of Abu Hanifa's statements he chuckled and said, "Regarding his claim that I am a reader, he is right. I read the books of my forefathers Abraham and Moses."

Sometime later as Imam Al-Sadiq sat with his companions, there was a knock on his door. One of the boys in the house would answer the door. He returned to the Imam to tell him that it was Abu Hanifa. "Let him in," the Imam

---

[4] Al-Sadouq, *'Ilal Al-Sharai'*, 1:89, H. 8.

said. Abu Hanifa entered and said his Salaam[5] to the Imam. The Imam responded in kind. "Do you permit me to sit?" asked Abu Hanifa. Imam Al-Sadiq did not respond to him and instead gave his attention to his companions. Abu Hanifa then asked a second and third time but was once again ignored. Abu Hanifa, nevertheless, sat down without the permission of the Imam. When the Imam noticed that he had sat down he turned to him and said, "You are the jurist of the people of Iraq?"

"Yes," replied Abu Hanifa.

"With what do you give them verdicts?"

"With the Book of God and the tradition of His Prophet."

"Abu Hanifa, so you truly know the Book of God, and the verses of abrogation and the abrogated verses?"

"Yes."

"O Abu Hanifa, you have claimed knowledge. Woe to you, God has not made that except for the People of the Book whom God revealed to. Woe to you, and that is not for anyone but the particular individuals from the progeny of our Prophet. God has not given you even a letter from His book. So if you are as you say – and you are not as you say – then tell me of the words of God, 'Travel through them in safety, night and day.'[6] Where is that on Earth?"

"I reckon that it is between Mecca and Medina."

---

5 Salaam or Al-Salaam Alaykum is the standard Muslim greeting meaning "Peace be upon you."

6 The Holy Quran, 34:18.

Imam Al-Sadiq then turned to his companions and said, "You do know that people are stopped between Mecca and Medina, robbed of their money, unable to save themselves and killed?" They responded in the affirmative. Abu Hanifa remained quiet.

"O Abu Hanifa, tell me of God's words, 'And whoever enters it shall be secure.'[7] Where is that place?"

"It is the Ka'ba."

"When Al-Hajjaj ibn Youssef launched his catapults on Ibn Zubayr while he was in the Ka'ba, killing him, was he safe?"

Abu Hanifa did not respond.

"O Abu Hanifa, if something is presented to you that is not in the Book of God nor is it in the heritage or tradition [of the Prophet] what do you do?"

"I analogize and judge based on my opinion."

"O Abu Hanifa, the first to analogize [as such] was the cursed Lucifer. He analogized with our Lord the Exalted and said, 'I am better than him. You created me from fire and You created him from clay.'[8]"

Abu Hanifa remained quiet and did not respond.[9]

Imam Al-Sadiq carried on with a series of questions leaving Abu Hanifa stupefied. In a gathering of deep and detailed discussion similar to this, Abu Hanifa would rise from his

---

7 The Holy Quran, 3:97.
8 The Holy Quran, 7:12.
9 Al-Sadouq, *'Ilal Al-Sharai'*, 1:89

seat to walk up to Imam Al-Sadiq and kiss his head saying, "The most knowledgeable of people... one whom we've never seen before a scholar." His statement was quite telling. Abu Hanifa, the "the Jurist of Iraq" could not help but acknowledge the Imam as the most knowledge of his time. It was not merely because of the Imam's superior knowledge and reason; rather, it was his approach of genuine care and compassion. He had this approach for a reason. He wanted to help people grow. He wished to reach their minds and souls in the most effective way possible, and that would be through his impeccable character combined with his irrefutable reason.

Imam Al-Sadiq made it a point to respectfully, objectively, and effectively address the claims of those posed themselves as scholars out to guide or lead the community of believers. Through his discourses he stressed the importance of solid arguments and logical reasoning. If you are to make a claim, you best be able to defend it with proof. The proof itself must be valid and not merely empty rhetoric and baseless assertions. Imam Al-Sadiq did not deride or neglect someone because they differed with him in views or beliefs, or if they were deviant in their own creed or philosophy. Rather, he shared his knowledge with whoever was willing and able to receive regardless of their background. During his time, the Muslim community had opened up to new horizons in knowledge and science. Be it exegesis of the Holy Quran, theology, ethics, jurisprudence, or the natural sciences, the Imam trained and taught thousands during his lifetime. He provided benefit and guidance to all. Abu Hanifa himself would go on to be the leader of one of the four jurisprudential schools of thought within Sunni Islam. Many of the Imams students would become scholars in their own right in subjects such as history, jurisprudence, theology, chemistry, astronomy and other sciences. His example was a manifestation of the words of God, "And that which profits the people stays in the earth."[10]

He cared about providing that necessary balance between gains in this life and securing one's wellbeing in the next. In any time of doubt between priority of activities or practice, he reiterated the words of God, "the Hereafter is better and more lasting."[11] Using reason one could not deny this and would realign his actions within this everlasting principle. It was this consistent culture of remembrance, logical reasoning, objective thinking that the Imam reinforced. Even more so, the Imam wanted to empower the idea of giving back and the potential of the individual. He enfranchised people to harness that potential and work on themselves to become the best they possibly could be. Even when he was threatened by those who wished to quell his influence and put an end to his following, he creatively navigated through those situations with ease and grace.

This was in a crucial period of political upheaval with the decline of the Umayyad and the rise of the Abbasids to the caliphate. This turbulent time, though it had its set of chal-

---

lenges, was seized by Imam Al-Sadiq as an opportunity to focus on teaching, education, and leading people through the proper guidance and scholarship of religion. It was this fine ability that Imam Al-Sadiq's possessed that allowed him to be the go-to source for scholars and people of all backgrounds and schools of thought.

> *People cited him in all sciences... as his reputation spread from country to country. The prominent scholars relayed narrations from him, as this included the likes of Yahya ibn Saeed, Ibn Jurayh, Al-Sufyanen, Abu Hanifa, Shu'ba, and Ayoub Al-Sakhtiyani.*[12]

Through his inclusive yet distinct and compassionate yet confident style of leadership, he embedded the fundamentals of ethics and human development in his society. He did so in such a way that would allow the generations after him would have a greater aptitude for development and advancement, building on what was already established by his forefathers. Imam Al-Sadiq's principles were consistent and what he spoke of was based on those principles. Society's wellbeing and success would be contingent on their commitment to the universal values that God bestowed upon humanity. Those values were their tools for attaining their success as individuals and as a collective community. He stressed the Book of God and what it brought of guidance, not simply in theory but in practice. "Indeed, it is an august Book: falsehood cannot approach it, at present or in future,

---

[12] Ibn Hajar, *Al-Sawa'iq Al-Muhriqa*, 2:586.

a [revelation gradually] sent down from One all-wise, all-laudable."[13] In that same vein, the Imam showed that his school of thought was a continuation of what the Holy Prophet established of principles and practices of excellence. For one, knowledge and ethics went hand in hand. There was a direct correlation with the pursuit of knowledge and the way one engaged with the rest of creation.

Imam Ali said, "Knowledge is tied to practice, for whoever knows will practice. Knowledge speaks through practice, it is either answered through it or leaves without it."[14] It is not enough to know or believe in a principle or idea. Development and progress comes through practicing that belief or principle. Real progress cannot be attained without that, instead the discussion will be limited to hopes and imagination instead of actualized potential.

Experts on principles of human development agree that development begins with ideas. However, they stress that ideas must be put into action. Habits cannot be changed without identifying both the principles and the actions that need to be reinforced. Identifying usually carries on from brainstorming to writing things down on paper and putting a plan together to implement that change and movement towards reform. Then actually implementing that plan, based on the principled contemplated, would result in that movement towards change and betterment. Both are needed – the ideas and the action. Without action the ideas remain

---

[13] The Holy Quran, 41:41 – 42.
[14] Al-Radi, *Nahjul Balagha*, 539, Saying 366.

abstract and have little to actual impact, and without the ideas the action has no guidance or objective and could be in lost energy exerted in vain. This is what the Imams stressed – this comprehensive approach embodied in balance and realizing the importance of all things practical and theoretical.

What made Imam Al-Sadiq's school of thought so unique was his impressive style of leadership and scholarship – one that was comprehensive in its approach to fulfilling humanity's destiny as the viceroy of God on Earth. Our potential is immense and the Imam dealt with people acknowledging that great potential they had. For it to be harnessed, however, they had to utilize the tools and habits that would best allow them to reach that potential and fulfill their fate. On seeking knowledge as one of the primary pursuits of excellence and virtue he said, "Rush towards seeking knowledge! By the One whom my soul is in His hands, one narration learned from an honest individual is better than this [whole] world and what it holds of gold and silver."[15] While he stressed pursuing knowledge, he emphasized that such a pursuit be done with an ethic of humbleness and humility.

"Be humble before those you learn from and be humble with those you teach."[16] He made sure his followers knew what seeking knowledge was all about, and that without purifying one's intention and outlook that knowledge would be in vain. No one should be disillusioned by the knowledge

---

[15] Al-Tabrasi, *Mishkat Al-Anwar*, 236, II. 673.
[16] Ibid, 242, II. 701.

they gain and even think of arrogance, conceit, or superiority because of their knowledge. Be it a teacher or a student, if humility is lost then there is no value in the knowledge gained. It is that humbleness that shows maturity, wisdom, and true progress from that knowledge.

From that humbleness one will also be more inclined not to flex every time a question comes his way. To answer every question a person is asked would be absurd. Imam Al-Sadiq said, "The one who answers every question they are asked is insane."[17] When asked about why he considers such an individual to be "insane" the Imam answered it is because, "One who is sane is a person who puts things in their proper place."[18] Hurrying to provide an answer to any and every question is not putting things in their proper place or order. We cannot possibly have all the answers all the time, and to assume such a position would be destructive. Saying "I don't know" or remaining silent instead of jumping to answer a question shows wisdom and maturity. Answering a question does not necessarily display knowledge or courage, just like silence is certainly not a sign of shame or weakness; rather, silence could be a show strength and confidence.

As part of the pursuit of knowledge, the Imam encouraged his followers to write, research, and engage in dialogue. It wasn't merely about taking what one learned but furthering it by documentation and spreading the knowledge with others.

---

[17] Al-Sadouq, *Ma'ani Al-Akhbar*, 238, II. 2.
[18] Ibid, 510, II. 235.

Write and share your knowledge with your brothers. When you die bequeath your books to your children. For there will be a time that will come where people will not be at ease except with their books.[19]

We have a responsibility towards one another as a community when it comes to knowledge and information. It starts with learning and documentation. That documentation can turn into published writings. Those writings are to be shared, preserved, and inherited from one generation to the next. The value of this needs to be acknowledged and upheld, lest it is neglected and the heritage of knowledge is lost. Without that development would be that much harder.

Moreover, our responsibility towards one another extends in all of the essential matters that we have discussed throughout this book. The ideas of human development, ethics, and leadership must be engrained in our psyche as we nourish our upcoming generations and prepare them for the challenges and successes they will face. Compassion, moderation, justice, and integrity are key principles that need be a part of our daily lives. We must incorporate these values into our practices where it is not merely an abstract idea of goodness, but a chosen habit developed and embedded in our thought and conduct. With these principles we can become closer to that great potential that God has for us. We become closer to our happiness and success in the life and the hereafter.

---

[19] Al-Kulayni, *Al-Kafi*, 1:52, H. 11.